c|net Do-It-Yourself

LAPTOP PROJECTS

24 cool things you didn't know you could do!

About the Authors

Justin Jaffe (Portland, Maine) is a former senior editor for CNET, where he managed the laptop reviews program. His writings, reviews, and recommendations have appeared in *BusinessWeek*, the *San Francisco Chronicle, Laptop, Computer Shopper*, and online at Wired.com.

Brian Nadel (New York) is a freelance writer and the former editor in chief of Mobile Computing & Communications magazine. A 25-year veteran of technology journalism, he has worked for *Popular Science, PC Magazine*, and *Business Tokyo*.

c|net Do-It-Yourself
LAPTOP PROJECTS

24 cool things you didn't know you could do!

Justin Jaffe
Brian Nadel

New York   Chicago   San Francisco
Lisbon   London   Madrid   Mexico City
Milan   New Delhi   San Juan
Seoul   Singapore   Sydney   Toronto

The McGraw·Hill Companies

McGraw-Hill books are available at special quantity discounts to use as premiums and sales promotions, or for use in corporate training programs. For more information, please write to the Director of Special Sales, Professional Publishing, McGraw-Hill, Two Penn Plaza, New York, NY 10121-2298. Or contact your local bookstore.

CNET Do-It-Yourself Laptop Projects:
24 Cool Things You Didn't Know You Could Do!

1234567890 QPD QPD 019876

ISBN-13: 978-0-07-226469-2
ISBN-10:   0-07-226469-1

Sponsoring Editor
Roger Stewart

Proofreader
Raina Trivedi

Art Director, Cover
Jeff Weeks

Editorial Supervisor
Jody McKenzie

Indexer
Kevin Broccoli

Cover Designer
Jeff Weeks

Project Manager
Vasundhara Sawhney

Production Supervisor
Jim Kussow

Cover Illustration
Sarah Howell

Acquisitions Coordinator
Carly Stapleton

Composition
International Typesetting and Composition

Technical Editors
Matthew Elliott

Illustration
International Typesetting and Composition

Copy Editor
Margaret Berson

In memory of Tom Wilson
—Justin Jaffe

For those who have put up with me:
Peter, Jamie, Amy and—of course—slowy.
—Brian Nadel

Contents at a Glance

Part III   Advanced

Contents

Part III   Advanced

Foreword

*P*ersonal computer: the phrase conjures images of a heavy, putty-grey box sitting on the floor, a bulky CRT monitor hogging a desktop, and the owner of both tethered to one place to use them. Then came the laptop.

Once upon a time notebooks were an extravagant alternative, owned almost exclusively by road warriors or the technically effete who would overlook the high prices and relatively low performance. What a difference a few years and few hundred dollars less makes. Today's laptop computer is the rock star of PCs, with ample power, skinny prices, and sales on a tear, whereas desktop computers raise the pulse only of those who don't have a computer at all. The laptop combines the power of computing, the freedom of wireless, the richness of the Internet, and the spontaneity of real life.

So, we present you with a range of DIY projects that will help make your laptop an even more essential and capable device. You'll learn how to perform hardware upgrades that seem daunting on a small machine (hint: they're not), and you'll discover creative projects that were once deemed too difficult for a portable computer, such as turning your VHS tapes into DVDs.

I hope you'll also find that the projects in this book salute an important attribute of the laptop: it puts the *personal* back in *personal computer*. Laptops are truly personal electronics; they hold our entertainment as well as our work and segue seamlessly between both. They are, simply, an accessory for living. Look over the projects in this book and you'll see how you can make that accessory enhance your life.

Brian Cooley
CNET Editor-at-Large

Acknowledgments

This book would not have been possible without participation from my co-author Brian Nadel; guidance from Roger Stewart at McGraw-Hill; help and advice from my former colleagues at CNET, especially Lindsey Turrentine, Matt Elliott, Eliot Van Buskirk, and Rafe Needleman; encouragement from my parents Gail and Michael and my brother Eric; and the unflagging support of my lovely wife Amy.

—Justin Jaffe

In addition to my creative co-author Justin Jaffe, I would like to acknowledge those people who helped me over the years to realize that the only limits that we place on computing are those that exist in our minds. Without their inspiration, I would never have tried to do any of the things described in this book. In a very real sense, this is their book.

—Brian Nadel

Introduction

Whatever type of laptop you have—big or small, new or old, fancy or not—it can do far more than you ever thought possible. E-mailing, surfing the Web, and word processing are great, but with the step-by-step directions in this book, we'll show you how to transform your laptop into a home stereo, a TiVo, or a home security system. You'll learn how to use your laptop to make free phone calls, navigate your way across the country, and DJ a party. And on top of all of that, we'll guide you through upgrading some of your laptop's internal components to make it run faster and more powerfully.

Who Is This Book For?

This book is for anyone who wants to take their laptop to the limit and get as much use and enjoyment out of it as possible. Neither computer knowledge nor high-tech know-how is required.

That means you. Read on.

Which Laptops Does This Book Cover?

Most of the projects in this book will work with almost any laptop running a recent version of Microsoft Windows, though some require additional hardware and software and slightly higher system requirements than others.

In general, if you have an Internet connection and your laptop has a CD drive and a few megabytes of free hard drive space, you're in business.

What Does This Book Cover?

This book consists of 24 separate projects, divided into three categories: Easy Projects, Challenging Projects, and Advanced Projects. Here are examples of what you'll find:

- **Easy Projects** Making a great car stereo; playing digital music on your home stereo; making free phone calls; transferring LPs and cassettes to CD or MP3s; starring in your own Internet TV show; and DJing a party.

- **Challenging Projects**   Watching and recording TV; transferring your home videos to DVD; using your fingerprints instead of passwords; protecting your data from disaster; navigating a roadtrip across the country or across your town.

- **Advanced Projects**   Building a home security system; cleaning your laptop (inside and out); and upgrading your laptop's components including the battery, operating system, memory, hard drive, and processor.

Each project is a self-contained unit, although some projects refer to steps in other projects to avoid repetition. Each project is divided into a number of major steps, with each step providing clear instructions on how to proceed.

You may choose to start with easy projects and move up to more ambitious projects. But the way the book is structured allows you to dive directly into any project that appeals to you.

Each project starts with a list of any extra hardware and software you need and an idea of the approximate cost, so you know exactly what you're getting into.

Conventions Used in This Book

To make its meaning clear, this book uses various conventions, two of which are worth mentioning here:

- Note, Tip, and Caution paragraphs highlight information you should pay extra attention to

- The pipe character or vertical bar denotes choosing an item from a menu. For example, "choose File | Open" means that you should pull down the File menu and select the Open item. Use the keyboard, mouse, or a combination of the two as you wish.

Part I

Easy

Project 1

Make a Killer Car Stereo

What You'll Need

- Hardware: FM transmitter, power adapter (optional)
- Software: Digital music player
- Cost: $5 to $30 U.S.

If you're like us, you've got hundreds (or thousands) of songs on your laptop. The problem is that you don't have any good way to get all of that rockin' into your car. Sure, you could burn all of those music files, 15 or so at a time, onto a bunch of CDs. But that would be time-consuming and expensive. The good news is that it's easy to turn your laptop into a full-featured car stereo jukebox.

Step 1: Find a Good Seat for Your Laptop

Your biggest decision will be where to put your laptop in your car. You'll want to find a spot that's secure and accessible to you while you're at the wheel—on your lap is not a good choice. If you're driving solo, we recommend that your laptop ride shotgun. And just to be extra careful, go ahead and fasten the seatbelt around it—you don't want your laptop flying around if you make a hard stop.

Depending on the size of your laptop (and your car), an open glove compartment can make a nice shelf (see Figure 1-1); the armrest between the front seats may work, too. A few pieces of Velcro adhesive will hold your laptop in place nicely.

Figure 1-1

The perfect place for a laptop.

Plug Right In

If your car stereo has a stereo input (see Figure 1-2) or RCA jacks, this project is a piece of cake.

Figure 1-2

An audio input in the glove compartment.

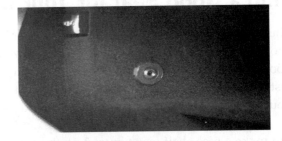

All you'll need is an audio cable (see Figure 1-3) that has mini stereo jacks at each end.

Figure 1-3

An audio cable.

Plug one end into the notebook's headphone connector (see Figure 1-4) and the other into the car stereo's input. Be sure that your audio cable is long enough to extend from the stereo to wherever your laptop will sit. This method generally delivers the highest audio quality.

Figure 1-4

The headphone jack.

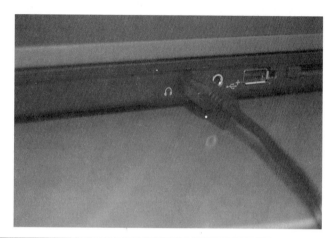

Step 2: Get Set to Transmit

If your car stereo doesn't have input jacks (or you're a neat freak who doesn't want wires running across the car), a small FM transmitter will transform your laptop into a radio station that can broadcast a short-range signal directly to your car's radio.

Plug the FM transmitter into the notebook's headphone jack (see Figure 1-5), and tune the car's radio to a vacant frequency where all you hear is static or nothing at all. Now, set the transmitter to the same frequency as the radio.

Figure 1-5

Plug the transmitter into the headphone jack.

tip *The key to a good FM transmission is finding a place on your car stereo's radio that has no station on it. Most FM transmitters work best at the bottom of the dial—between 88 and 90 MHz—where there are fewer stations and what stations there are usually broadcast at a low wattage that won't interfere with your signal.*

Step 3: Load Up Some Tunes

Now that everything's connected, we're almost there. Because it comes preloaded on most laptops, we're going to use Microsoft Windows Media Player, but there are plenty of other free digital music player applications available; for up-to-date reviews and recommendations, check out www.download.com. Start by dragging the music you want into Windows Media Player's interface (see Figure 1-6). Click the play button and you should hear the music coming out of your car stereo's speakers.

Figure 1-6

Drag your music files right into the Media Player.

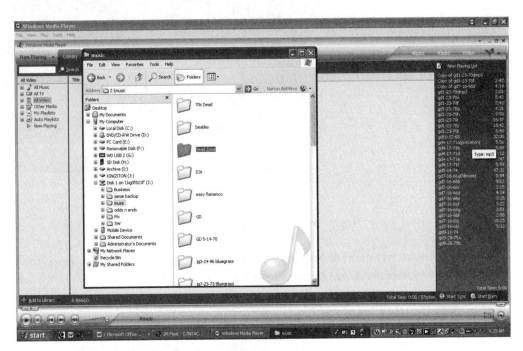

> **note** Your laptop can store about 2,500 songs for every 10GB it has of free hard drive space. If you've got 60GB of music on your laptop, that comes out to about 10,000 tunes—enough to play continuously for about a month, 24 hours a day, without ever repeating one.

Step 4: Set the Vibe

Windows Media Player has a processor that can adjust the audio for the speakers in your car. Go into the *Tools* menu and select *Options* (see Figure 1-7). Click on the *Devices* tab and select *Speakers*; in the *Sound Playback* area, click the *Advanced* button. Now, in the *Speaker Settings* area, again, click the *Advanced* button. From the *Speaker Setup* drop-down list, select whichever setting sounds best in your car.

Figure 1-7

Optimize your sound.

> **tip** *Laptop batteries are notoriously short-lived, so before you set out on a long journey, we recommend getting an adapter that will draw power from your car's cigarette lighter to keep your stereo juiced. Most laptop manufacturers make special car kits for their own models, and third-party vendors such as Kensington and Targus make adapters that will work with most laptops.*

When you're driving, it's smart to keep your eyes on the road. Otherwise, you might die. Unless you've already set up a playlist or set your music player program to random, we suggest letting your navigator play DJ. If you're alone in the car, pull over or wait for a red light before you queue up the next song.

> **tip** *Though the arrangement differs from one keyboard model to another, the function keys at the top of your keyboard often double as shortcuts for various audio functions. For example, F9 and F10 generally lower and raise the volume, and F8 mutes it. Get to know your function keys.*

Project 2

Build a Wireless Network

What You'll Need

- Hardware: Linksys WRT54GS wireless router, broadband Internet connection, two Ethernet cables
- Software: Included
- Cost: $10 to $200 U.S.

In this chapter, we'll show you how to build a wireless network for your home. It'll give you the freedom to surf the Internet and send e-mail from anywhere—your kitchen, bedroom, even the back yard. Setting up a wireless network is easy to do, and will give you a leg up on some of the other projects in this book.

note *The various wireless networking standards make about as much sense as a bowl of alphabet soup. But since you asked: The first protocol, 802.11b, delivers approximately 5 to 11 megabits per second (Mbps) of data and has a range of approximately 300 feet. The second protocol, 802.11a, delivers higher data speeds, but has a much shorter range and uses a different frequency, which has cost it popularity. The 802.11g protocol, a variant of 802.11b, can deliver 54Mbps and is compatible with 802.11b equipment. The newest standard, 802.11n, promises superior speed and range; using multiple antennas, 802.11n routers are compatible with both 802.11b and 802.11g devices and can deliver more than 200Mbps. Confused? Check out www.cnet.com for advice on which wireless router and networking standard are the best for you.*

Although setting up a wireless network isn't rocket science, there are a number of details—keys, codes, and names—that you'll need to remember and refer to during the course of this and other projects. At the end of this chapter, we've included a place for you to record these details. When you're done with this project, all of the information you'll ever need about your wireless network will be right there in this book.

To build our wireless network, we'll be using a Linksys WRT54GS wireless router, which operates on the 802.11g format. OK, let's cut the cords.

Step 1: Insert the CD

Insert the CD that came with your wireless router into the laptop's drive. Most router software will give you the option to open a user guide; you definitely don't have to read it, but it can't hurt to print it, so you'll have it if something ever goes wrong. Now, click *Start Setup* to begin (see Figure 2-1).

Figure 2-1

Print the manual and then start the setup.

Step 2: Connect the Modem

Connect one end of the Ethernet cable to the router and the other to your cable or DSL modem (see Figure 2-2). Don't turn the router on yet.

Figure 2-2

Connect the router to your cable or DSL box.

Step 3: Take It Easy

Linksys's EasyLink Advisor program will now walk us through the steps to building a wireless network. You answer the questions, and it'll set up the networking parameters.

After you accept the software license and load the program, the Linksys software will ask you to pick a name for your network. Choose a word that you won't easily forget—we'll use *plastics*—and type it into the *Network Name* box (see Figure 2-3).

Figure 2-3

One word for you—"plastics."

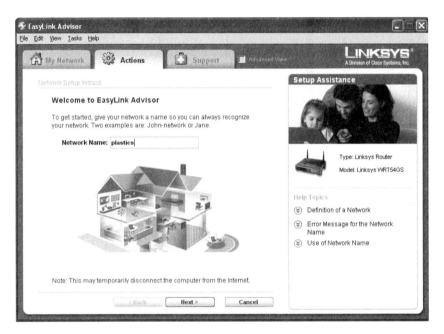

After you've recorded your network name in the allotted space at the end of this chapter, click *Next*.

Step 4: Silver or Blue?

On the next screen, you'll be asked to tell the software what color your router is (see Figure 2-4). It sounds a bit silly, but it will help the software determine which router model you're using. Ours is blue.

Step 5: Connect the Router

When prompted (see Figure 2-5), turn on the router by plugging in its AC adapter; the LEDs will light up and blink on and off. Once they've settled down, using the second Ethernet cable, connect your laptop to the router.

Figure 2-4

What color is your router?

Figure 2-5

Go ahead, plug it in.

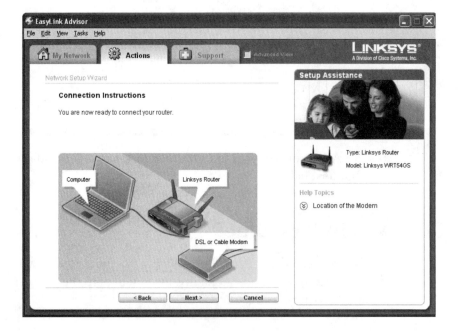

A number of LEDs should now be glowing green or blinking: Power, WLAN, one of the four Ethernet ports, and Internet (see Figure 2-6). Once your lights are lit, click *Next*.

Figure 2-6

Make sure the correct lights are on.

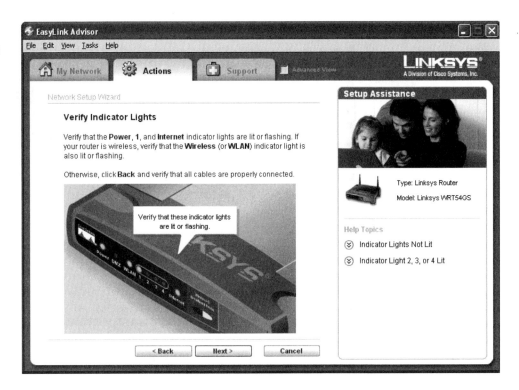

<tip> If your lights aren't lit—or if you get stuck at any point during this setup process—click on Show Me How. The software will play a brief explanatory cartoon. The explanations are basic, but helpful if you're just not getting it.

Step 6: Find That Router

The software will now automatically begin configuring the router (see Figure 2-7). If it doesn't detect it immediately, don't fret. Try again.

Step 7: Secure Your Network

After the program detects your router, it will prompt you to configure your security settings. Unbelievably, most people don't secure their network. They'd never leave their front door unlocked, but they leave their wireless network open to anyone with a WiFi-equipped computer.

Well, not on our watch. We'll be securing our network from snoops, hackers, and neighbors who want to piggyback on our broadband connection. Click to secure the network (see Figure 2-8).

Figure 2-7

Searching…

Figure 2-8

Call in security.

> **note**   *Wireless network security encryption comes in two flavors: Wired Equivalent Privacy (WEP) and WiFi Protected Access (WPA). Just about every router, laptop, and PC Card supports WEP. WPA, the newer and more secure standard, isn't always supported by older devices.*

Step 8: WEP It Up

We're going to use 128-bit WEP encryption to keep our network simple, secure, and compatible with a bunch of our older gear.

The EasyLink software will automatically create an encryption key for you.

Step 9: Get Checked

OK, it's the moment of truth. Unplug the Ethernet cable from your laptop. Let the software check your connection (see Figure 2-9). Once you see the little green check marks, you're in good shape.

Figure 2-9

All checked and ready.

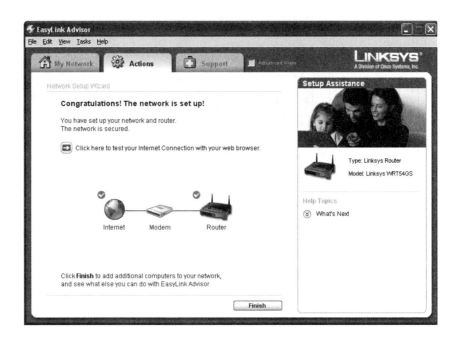

Step 10: Find Your Router a Home

Now that it's set up, we must find a home for your router, and proper placement is critical. You'll want to find a space that's near an AC outlet and your cable or DSL box. To get maximum range, find a high area that's near the center of your home and that's unobstructed by stone, brick, or heavy plaster walls. Choice locations may include a high shelf of a bookcase (see Figure 2-10), on top of the refrigerator, or even in a closet.

tip *If your connection is weak, try repositioning the router's antennas. Also make sure that it's not too close to a microwave oven or wireless phone—devices that may interfere with the router's signal.*

As with any radio transmitter, signal strength—and data flow—depend on how far the laptop is from the router. When the two are next to each other, you'll get top speed; at a distance, you'll see a slower rate.

Figure 2-10

A bookshelf is a great place to stash a router.

Step 11: Connect Another Laptop

Now that your wireless network is set up, your friends and roommates are going to want to get in on the action. EasyLink will prompt you to choose a connection type for an additional computer. You should select—big surprise—wireless (see Figure 2-11).

Figure 2-11

Uh, we're going wireless.

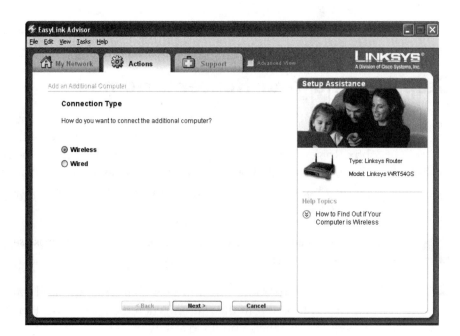

Step 12: Set Up a Wireless Connection

Now the software will prompt you to download the setup file, which you'll want to put onto your buddy's laptop. The easiest way to get it there is to connect his laptop directly to the router using an Ethernet cable.

Once your buddy's laptop is connected, have him open a Web browser, type in www.linksysfix.com/ela, and double-click the installation icon, and the File Download dialog box will appear (see Figure 2-12).

Figure 2-12

Hey buddy, download the software from Linksys's web site.

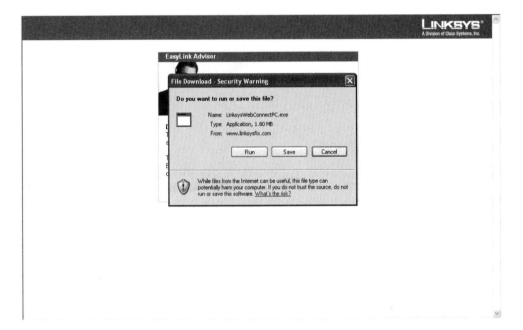

Now open the software. Click *Next* to configure the wireless connection (see Figure 2-13). This basic software is all it takes to connect new computers; you might even want to put it on a USB drive or burn it to a CD, which will make it easy to quickly add a new PC.

Step 13: Check Out the Wireless Wonder

Nice. Now you and your friend should be surfing wirelessly on your new wireless network.

tip *Wonder how fast your Internet connection is? Check out the free bandwidth meter at www.cnet.com.*

Step 14: Locate Your Settings

To access your wireless network's configuration settings, open a Web browser and type in the router's home address (192.168.1.1). The user name and password will both be set to "admin." We recommend that you change those before you do anything

Figure 2-13

EasyLink will teach any PC how to connect to the network.

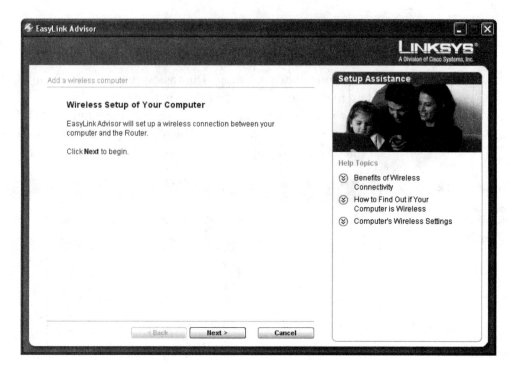

else; you can record the user name and password in the space at the end of this chapter. Now go to the *Wireless* tab and click on *Security* to see your encryption key (see Figure 2-14). Write that down, too.

Figure 2-14

The router's Wireless settings page has lots of detailed information about the settings.

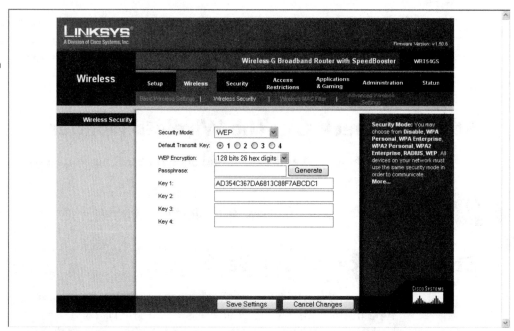

Add Wireless Networking to Your Laptop

If your laptop doesn't have built-in wireless, don't cry; it's easy and inexpensive to add it. All you need is a wireless networking PC Card. We'll use an old D-Link DWL-G650 card that we picked up on the cheap.

The first step is to load the included software from the CD that came with the card. Install the software, restart your laptop, and you'll see a desktop icon for the PC Card wireless radio.

Now slide the card into the PC Card slot (see Figure 2-15). You'll notice a new icon in the taskbar, with a large "I" in the middle; right-click on it and choose *Advanced Configuration*.

Figure 2-15

Plug the card into the PC Card slot.

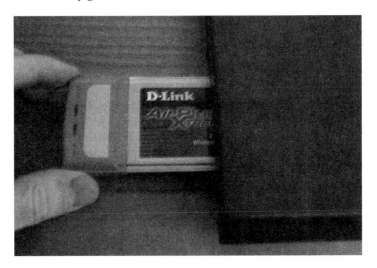

Pick a name for your profile and fill in your network's information (see Figure 2-16). Now select the *Encryption* tab, and type in your encryption key; the software masks the actual key as you type it. When you're finished, the icon in the taskbar will turn green—now the router and your laptop are connected wirelessly.

Figure 2-16

Fill in the information about your network.

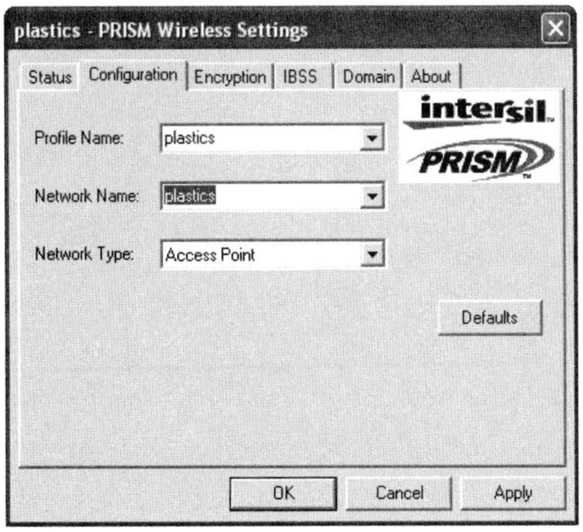

Your Wireless Network Information

Fill in the following form with your network's details for future reference.

Router model	
User name	
Password	
IP address	
Network name	
Encryption type	
Encryption key	

Play Digital Music on Your Home Stereo

What You'll Need

- Hardware: Home stereo, 3.5 mm stereo cable or 3.5 mm-to-dual-RCA male adapter and dual RCA cable or optical cable, wireless network and network digital audio bridge (optional)
- Software: Digital music player
- Cost: $5 to $80 U.S.

With so much music available online—everything from Abba to Z-Trip, not to mention Internet radio and podcasts–wouldn't it be nice if you could play it all on your home stereo? After all, even the cheesiest home stereo has a better amplifier and speakers than the most expensive laptop. Fortunately, connecting your laptop to your home stereo requires only a few inexpensive cables; we'll show you how to do this first.

Of course, if you want to get fancy—and we think you do—you can connect your laptop to your home stereo wirelessly using a network digital audio receiver. It's a bit more complicated and will cost a few bucks more, but you'll be able to control your stereo remotely from anywhere in your home, and do it all without running a single wire. We'll show you how to do it in the second part of this chapter.

The Wired Way

Step 1: Check Out Your Connections

The type of stereo you have, and the kinds of connections it can accommodate, will determine which cables you'll need to use. Most home stereos have at least one pair of RCA inputs (see Figure 3-1) for connecting auxiliary components; if yours doesn't, see *Hook Up Another Way*. You'll need a cable that has a male 3.5 mm stereo jack at one end and a pair of male RCA connectors at the other (see Figure 3-2), which you should be able to pick up at a Radio Shack or a local hardware or electronics store.

Figure 3-1

RCA inputs.

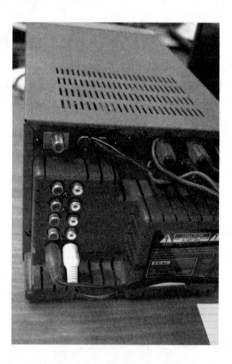

Figure 3-2

This cable is the key.

Hook Up Another Way

If you've got a cheap home stereo, or even just a boom box, and you can't find any RCA inputs, don't sweat it. If the stereo has a line-in jack, you can still get hooked up.

All you'll need is one 3.5 mm stereo cable. Just plug one end of the cable into your laptop's headphone jack and the other end into the stereo's line-in jack.

Step 2: Get Connected

Your stereo may have more than one set of RCA inputs for connecting to various other components such as a CD or DVD player or tape deck. Many stereo receivers also have auxiliary inputs, which are often labeled Aux (see Figure 3-3).

Figure 3-3

Auxiliary inputs.

If your stereo doesn't have auxiliary inputs, you can also connect to any other pair of inputs; if you use the tape inputs, however, connect to the "play" jacks, not the "record" jacks. Once you're hooked up, set your stereo to play from whichever input you plugged into; most home stereo receivers have a dial or switch that toggles the input source (see Figure 3-4).

Figure 3-4

Select the right source.

tip   *Be sure to plug the white RCA cable (left channel) into the white jack and the red RCA cable (right channel) into the red RCA jack.*

Finally, plug the 3.5 mm end of the cable into your laptop's headphone jack.

note   *Some higher-end laptops can connect to home audio components using lasers! If your laptop has an optical jack (see Figure 3-5), it can transmit a digital audio signal over a special fiber optic cable, which will deliver superbly clear, rich audio without any static or interference. Optical jacks are sometimes labeled Toslink or S/PDIF, which stands for Sony/Philips Digital Interface Format. Optical cables are expensive, but the sound quality is worth it.*

Figure 3-5

An S/PDIF (aka Toslink)
jack.

Step 3: Load Up Some Tunes

Now that everything's connected, we're almost there. Because it comes preloaded on most laptops, we're going to use Microsoft Windows Media Player, but there are plenty of other free digital music player applications available; for up-to-date reviews and recommendations, check out www.download.com. Start by dragging the music you want into Media Player's interface (see Figure 3-6). Click the play button and you should hear the music coming out of your home stereo's speakers. Voilà!

Figure 3-6

Drag files into the
music player.

The Wireless Way

You might not be crazy about the idea of tethering your laptop to your home stereo—after all, you got your laptop because it's portable. A network digital audio bridge can connect your laptop to your home stereo over a wireless network, so that your laptop can play music on the stereo from anywhere in (or around) your home. There are a number of great products on the market; we'll use the Linksys WMB54G Wireless-G Music Bridge to demonstrate.

Step 1: Install the Bridge

Start by loading the bridge's software onto your laptop from the included CD. After everything's installed and you've plugged the audio bridge into your laptop using the included LAN cable, the laptop should be able to automatically find the device and configure it. If you're unsure of what to do, consult the audio bridge manual.

tip *Don't worry if the laptop and audio bridge don't connect on the first try. Check the cables, but make sure the bridge is turned on and that the power and Ethernet lights are lit. It may take a few tries, but they should eventually find each other.*

Step 2: Configure the Bridge

Every vendor's audio bridge is a little different, but they all transmit your tunes over the wireless network to your stereo. Before the bridge can do that, however, you need to supply it with a few important details about your laptop and your network. You're going to need to supply the bridge with your wireless network's name and password (if you use one), and point it to where the music is stored on your laptop. Once you've shown the bridge how to access your network, you can disconnect the LAN cable. Again, specific directions on how to do this should be found in the audio bridge manual.

Step 3: Connect the Bridge to the Stereo

Next, launch the audio bridge's connection interface (see Figure 3-7).

Figure 3-7

Launch the bridge's software.

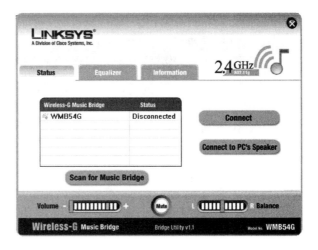

Now plug one end of the RCA cables into the bridge, and the other end into the stereo's *Aux* input. Congratulations! Your bridge has been built. Now it's time to send some music across it.

Step 4: Find That Confounded Bridge

Every audio bridge is a little different, but you'll need to have your laptop find the active music bridge and connect to it wirelessly. Once your laptop finds your bridge (see Figure 3-8), you're all set.

Figure 3-8

Ready to play.

Step 5: Load Up Some Tunes

Now that everything's connected, we're almost there. Because it comes preloaded on most laptops, we're going to use Microsoft Windows Media Player, but there are plenty of other free digital music player applications available; for up-to-date reviews and recommendations, check out www.download.com. Start by dragging the music you want into Media Player's interface. Click the play button and you should hear the music coming out of your home stereo's speakers. With most audio bridges, you can stray up to 100 feet away, and the music will still come through loud and clear. Good times.

tip *Your network digital audio bridge may have a built-in graphic equalizer that can tweak the sound to suit the type of music and the size and shape of the room. In addition to settings for rock, classical, and a slew of other styles, you can modify it to boost the high end or flatten the bass.*

When using a network digital audio receiver, keep in mind that there are range limits, and if your laptop strays too far from the wireless network, the rocking will come to a stop. If you need to roam further than your bridge will allow, try a powered antenna or signal booster for some additional range.

Print Wirelessly

What You'll Need

- Hardware: Wireless network, printer, wireless print server
- Software: Included
- Cost: $75 U.S.

Cords. Cables. Wires. We hate 'em. We do not enjoy having our laptop bound to Ethernet cords, phone cables, or printer wires. When we plug our laptop in to recharge the batteries, we weep. We just think that cables defeat the whole purpose of having a laptop.

If you already have a wireless network set up, you know how awesome it is to surf wirelessly (if not, learn how in Project 2). Even better, you're halfway to ridding yourself of those chains—OK, wires—that bind you to your printer.

To set your laptop up to print wirelessly, we'll be installing a print server, which will send data from your laptop to your printer. After this project, you'll be able to print from anywhere your network reaches—your bedroom, your backyard, wherever. Of course, you'll still have to retrieve the documents from your printer, unless you have an especially well-trained dog (or cat).

For this project, we'll be using the Linksys WPS11 Wireless-B Print Server, one of many options on the market, and our trusty HP LaserJet 1100 printer.

note *The letter "b" in the name of our printer server stands for 802.11b. The alphabet soup of wireless network specifications—802.11a, b, g, n, and others—is far too confusing and ridiculous to discuss at length. To make a long story short, while they might not be as fast as devices using the newer specs, 802.11b devices offer the widest compatibility with other 802.11 devices.*

Step 1: Set Up the Printer Server

First, load the CD that came with the printer server. It contains the drivers and admin software (see Figure 4-1).

Once you've installed the software, go to the Linksys web site (www.linksys.com) to see if any driver updates are available (see Figure 4-2).

Figure 4-1

Find the software for your print server.

Figure 4-2

Download and install the latest update.

Step 2: Make the Connection

Now go ahead and connect the server to the printer using a parallel cable (see Figure 4-3).

Figure 4-3

The last printer wire you'll ever need.

Step 3: Address Your Server

Out of the box, this printer server is set to a static IP address of 192.168.0.78. You can change the IP address using the Bi-Admin interface or set your entire network to use dynamic host configuration (DHCP), which lets your network router assign IP addresses to all devices on your network automatically. Either way works fine.

note *An Internet Protocol (IP) address lets devices identify and communicate with each other on a network. Any participating network device—such as your laptop and your printer server—must have its own unique address. A device's IP address can be thought of as its street address or phone number on the Internet.*

Step 4: Seek and Ye Shall Find

After your print server is set up on the network and connected to your printer, the Linksys software will scan the network for connected servers. If the server doesn't find anything on the first try, click *Refresh* to try again. Still not working? Unplug the server and give it a minute. Plug it back in and try again.

Still no connection? We're not out of ideas yet. Use a networking cable to physically connect the server to your router; now try again. You might need to configure the device while physically connected before setting it free.

tip *In some cases, you may need to reset the server's configuration. Push the button on the back of the server marked Reset and hold it for a count of ten. When you let go, it should start back up (now set to the factory default settings), and be ready to go.*

Step 5: Add Your New Printer

Once you've connected the server to the network, the Linksys print server software will pop up and ask if you want to add a new printer. Sounds good to us. Click *Add new printer*.

Now the Windows printer wizard will pop up. Select your printer maker and model from the drop-down lists and let the software load the drivers (see Figure 4-4). If you have the disk that came with the printer, you can use the drivers on it by clicking the *Have Disk...* button.

Figure 4-4

Pick your printer from the list.

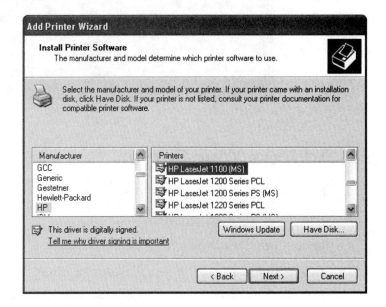

Step 6: Go Ahead, Be Selfish

Next, the Windows printer wizard will ask us whether we want to share our printer with other network users via Windows printer-sharing software. Doing so would require that documents be routed through at least one computer that's directly connected to the printer—and that won't work for us. We want to print directly from the laptop to the printer. So we'll select Do not share this printer (see Figure 4-5).

Step 7: Give It a Whirl

Now the wizard will ask to print a test page (see Figure 4-6). Sure, let's try it. Click Yes | Next.

Figure 4-5

Mine, mine, mine!

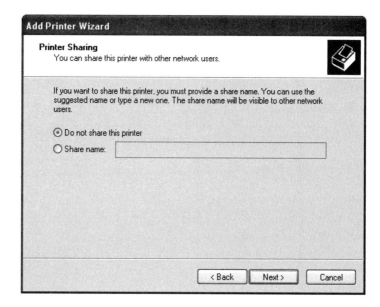

Figure 4-6

Print a test page.

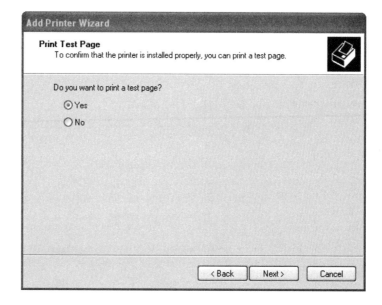

Step 8: Congratulate Yourself

If the page printed, congratulations! You're connected. Now open up the Bi-Admin interface and click the check box for TCP/IP protocol (see Figure 4-7).

Figure 4-7

Select your protocol.

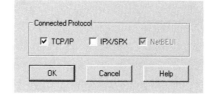

The program will now scan the network for print servers and, hopefully, find yours (see Figure 4-8).

Figure 4-8

Searching...

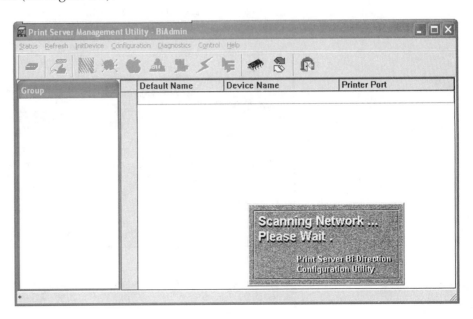

Connecting to a Secure Network

If your wireless network is configured for WEP (Wired Equivalent Privacy) or WPA (Wireless Protected Access), your life is more complicated but also more secure. Open Bi-Admin's Wireless Configuration dialog box, and fill in your network's name, channel number, type of security, and the all-important encryption key (see Figure 4-9). Be careful—the smallest typing error will prevent your server from connecting.

Figure 4-9

Add in your security settings.

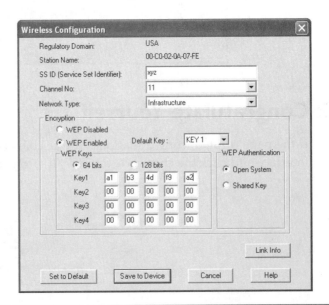

When you're done, click on *Link Info*. You'll want to see that the State is *Associated* (see Figure 4-10) and that the link quality and signal strength are in good shape.

Figure 4-10

Check on your connection.

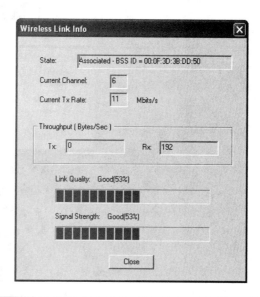

Step 9: Print from Anywhere

Now you can print from anywhere—as long as you're in range of your network.

Step 10: Cut to the Chase

Now that you're set up, you really don't have to deal with Linksys's Bi-Admin software any more. Just open any up-to-date web browser and type in your server's IP address (see Figure 4-11). Enter your password and you'll have access to tons of configuration details.

Step 11: Choose Options in the Print Server

The tabs are fairly self-explanatory: Server, Printer, TCP/IP, Wireless, and Status. The Advanced tab lets you set up printing on an AppleTalk network, among other things.

Step 12: Save Yourself

Just to be safe, we recommend that you save your settings using the Bi-Admin's Status menu; just click on *Backup/Restore Device Information* and save the file somewhere on your laptop. Also, it couldn't hurt to print the info—using your new wireless printer—and keep it with the manual. Go to Diagnostics and click Print Test Page. You'll get a nice printout of all of the configuration data (see Figure 4-12).

Figure 4-11

An IP address is all you need to tap into the server's setup page.

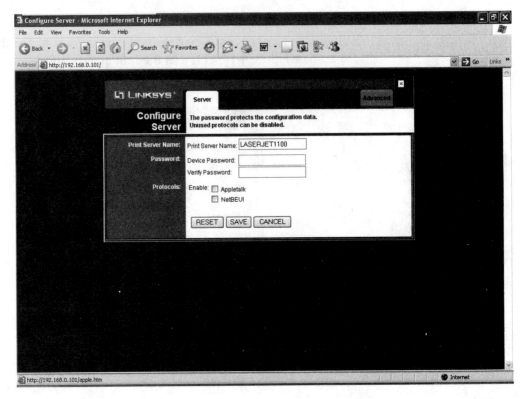

Now go back to your easy chair and print to your heart's content. Until the printer paper runs out...

Figure 4-12

Print the server's vital info for future reference.

```
Hardware ID: 0480568C2C
Firmware Version: 6026
Protocol ID: 807F
Default Name: SC0A07FE
Server Name: LASERJET1100
AppleTalk Info:
  Printer Type:
  LASERJET1100:LaserWriter
TCP/IP Info:
  IP Address: 192.168.0.110
  Subnet Mask: 255.255.255.0
  Gateway Address: 192.168.0.1
  Email Server IP Address: 0.0.0.0
  Printing Account Name:  N/A
  Redirect Account Name:  N/A
SMB Info:
  Domain Name:
WIRELESS Info:
  Station Name:00-06-25-0A-07-FE
  SSID:seilroc
  BSSID:00:0F:3D:3B:DD:50
  Channel No:6
  Network Type:Infrastructure
  Primary Firmware:PK010100.HEX
  Secondary Firmware:SF010402.HEX
```

Surf the Web on Your TV

What You'll Need

- Hardware: TV, Composite video or S-Video cable, RF modulator (optional), Bluetooth keyboard, and mouse (optional)
- Cost: $10 to $50 U.S.

The best thing about your laptop is that it's portable: the keyboard, the display—it's all built in and ready to go anywhere. The downside is that, with most laptops, the keyboard and display are considerably smaller than the full-sized versions you're accustomed to using with a regular desktop PC. And some activities—sharing photos, watching online videos, and even reading the online edition of the newspaper—just aren't cut out for a tiny screen.

Of course, you can always connect your laptop to a full-size keyboard (via a USB port) and connect to an external monitor (via a VGA or DVI output). Or, if you don't have a CRT or LCD monitor, you can hook up your laptop directly to your television.

If the TV was made in the last few years, there's a good chance it has *Composite video* and/or *S-video* inputs, which will make this project very simple. If you're stuck with an old hand-me-down TV, you'll probably need to buy an inexpensive *RF modulator*, which will let you connect your laptop via the TV's antenna cable port. Either way, this project should take no more than 10 minutes.

Step 1: Identify Your Connections

For this project, we're using a laptop that has a Composite video output (see Figure 5-1), which almost always looks like a yellow RCA jack; fortunately, just about every recent TV supports this connection. Most DVD players are hooked up to the TV via a Composite video connection, so you may need to disconnect that before you go any further.

Figure 5-1

Our laptop's
Composite jack.

Your laptop may also have an S-Video port (see Figure 5-2), though fewer TVs have an S-Video input; you'll need both to make this connection work.

Figure 5-2

An S-Video port.

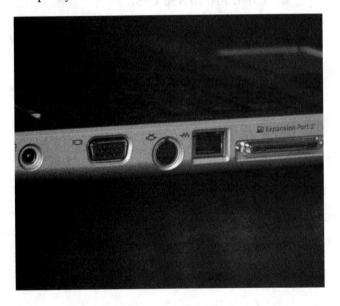

Also, beware that S-Video does not carry audio, so you'll need to make another connection if you want to hear Internet audio on your TV.

note *Inexpensive S-Video cables are notorious for degrading the signals considerably when transmitted across distances of more than 15 feet. We recommend buying the second-cheapest S-Video cable in the store (and we recommend a similar technique when buying wine in a restaurant).*

If you've got an older TV, you may not be able to find either of these newfangled S-Video or Composite video jacks on it. But you don't need 'em anyway, Grandpa. Go to an electronics store and buy an inexpensive *RF modulator*. It will convert your laptop's S-Video or Composite video signal into an RF signal that can be plugged straight into your TV's coaxial jack (see Figure 5-3). If you've got cable, it's probably connected to the TV via the coaxial port.

Figure 5-3

A TV coaxial jack.

Step 2: Wire for Audio and Video

As its name suggests, a Composite video connection transmits video only, so you'll need a special hybrid cable to bring audio and video from the laptop to the TV. This special cable has, at one end, a male composite video connector and a male 3.5 mm audio connector, and at the other end, three male RCA connectors (see Figure 5-4) that will plug into the TV's audio and video jacks. There are such cables available on the market, but they can be pricey. Instead of buying this special cable, however, we made our own from three other cables: a three-headed RCA cable (with one red, white, and yellow male end); a two-headed RCA cable that's female on both ends; and an RCA to 3.5 mm audio cable adapter. It'll work just as well as the special cable, though it'll be a bit messier. We recommend you use twist ties or Velcro straps to keep it from turning into a tangled mess. And remember to hook up to the correct colors: red for the right channel and white for the left.

Figure 5-4

Our home-made cable: at one end, one RCA connector and one 3.5 mm audio connector; at the other, three RCA connectors.

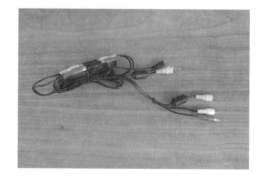

Step 3: Hook Up to Your TV

Newer TVs often have a set of input jacks accessible up front, sometimes behind a little door (see Figure 5-5). Otherwise, the inputs will be located in the back. You'll want to connect the three heads of the RCA cable to these inputs. Then, connect the loose yellow end to your laptop's Composite video port. Next, attach the two-headed RCA cable to the free ends of the three headed-cable (the white and red ends). Finally, connect the adapter to the two loose ends, and plug the 3.5 mm end into your laptop's headphone or line-out jack.

Figure 5-5

Behind door number one; our TV's input jacks.

Step 4: Bring Your TV Online

Turn on your laptop, and open up a web browser or any other application. You'll want to put something recognizable on the screen, so that you can confirm that your laptop is sending the signal to the TV.

 If your home's Ethernet or modem jacks are located close to the TV, you shouldn't have much trouble placing your laptop nearby. If they're across the room or somewhere else in the home entirely, you'll either need to buy a longer cable or set up a wireless network.

Step 5: Fine-Tune Your Laptop

Now that all of the connections have been made, you'll probably need to do a little tweaking to get all of the hardware and software cooperating with one another. Right-click anywhere on the Desktop and select *Properties* on the menu. Next, click the *Settings* tab. You'll see a big blue box labeled "1" and a smaller blue box labeled "2". Click the box marked "2"—that'll set your laptop to transmit to the external monitor; in this case, your TV.

You'll also want to adjust the resolution. Most TVs support much lower resolutions than a typical laptop, so try *640 by 480* or *800 by 600* first, and then move it up if the picture looks fuzzy. Next, click the *Advanced* button in the lower-right corner, select the *Monitor* tab, and choose *Generic TV* from the Monitor Type drop-down list (see Figure 5-6).

Figure 5-6

Select Generic TV.

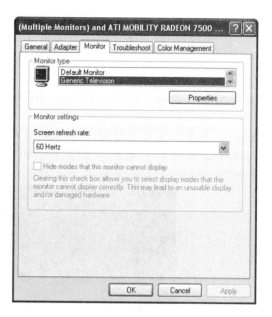

> **note** With the exception of the latest high-definition models, TVs are generally limited to much lower resolutions than laptops, and can often only show half as much information at one time. Your TV may be capable of displaying less than your laptop display, even if the TV screen is larger.

Step 6: Talk to Your TV

Now you need to tell your TV which signal to display, and just about every set works a little differently. Yours may have an Input switch on the front. Or you may need to tune to Channel 3 or 4. With some newer TVs, you'll need to use the remote control; look for a button called *Input* (see Figure 5-7).

Figure 5-7

Cycle through your TV's inputs until you find the right one.

Step 7: Send Video to the TV

It's time to give your laptop screen a rest; you'll need to tell the laptop to stop sending its video to its own screen and route it through whichever video connection you used in Step 1. Though most laptops can send the signal to their own screen and the TV simultaneously, the image looks better if you send it to the TV only. Look for the function key with the monitor icon on it (see Figure 5-8), and press it. The image on your laptops display should appear on your TV screen (see Figure 5-9).

Figure 5-8

This function key sends the signal to an external monitor; in this case, your TV.

Figure 5-9

Viola! Now playing on your TV--the Internet.

Now that you're connected to the TV, wouldn't it be nice to surf the web from your couch? A Bluetooth wireless keyboard and mouse will liberate you from your laptop and give you approximately 15 to 20 feet of range, just right for couch-potato surfing or gaming (see Figure 5-10).

Figure 5-10

Sit back and surf the wireless way.

Project 6

Make Free Phone Calls

What You'll Need:

- Hardware: Broadband Internet connection, speakers, microphone, USB or Bluetooth headset, webcam (optional)
- Software: Skype
- Cost: Free to $100 U.S.

We're going to show you how to use your laptop and a broadband Internet connection to kiss the phone company, its expensive services, and those horribly confusing bills goodbye. Go ahead—mwah! You're about to join the droves of people who have ditched traditional phone service for Voice over Internet Protocol (VoIP, pronounced voy-p).

Despite its inelegant name, VoIP has a lot to offer. First, with a few qualifications, it lets you make phone calls for free. Whether you're calling your uncle in Georgia or your auntie in Guam, you pay nothing. Second, you can take your phone number with you wherever you go. Whether you're moving from one city to another, staying in a hotel for business, or taking a weekend trip, you'll always make and take your calls at the same number. And there are other advantages, too, such as choosing your own area code, dialing phone numbers directly from Outlook, and using a webcam to make video calls.

We'll discuss how to do all these things later; first, let's get VoIP set up on your laptop. Though there are a number of proficient Internet phone services, we'll use our favorite, Skype, to demonstrate.

note Voice over Internet Protocol—*also called VoIP (and pronounced voyp), IP Telephony, Internet Telephony, and Broadband Phone—is the routing of voice conversations over the Internet instead of traditional dedicated telephone transmission lines. Instead of plugging a handset into a phone jack, your voice travels over a web-connected network. In short, it's like instant messaging with your voice instead of text.*

Skype can be used with all of the major operating systems—Windows, Mac, and Linux—as well as with a variety of handhelds and smart phones. The basic premise is that you can call anyone else who uses Skype for free—and with more than 100 million subscribers, that may include an ever-increasing number of your friends and family. Of course, you can still call people who don't have Skype—and it'll cost you only a few cents a minute, no matter where in the world you're calling.

Step 1: Download the Software

Your first step into the liberating world of VoIP is to get the Skype software. It's free, which is nice. Go to Skype's web site (www.skype.com) and click on the *Download* link. After selecting whichever operating system you're using, click the *Get it now* button (see Figure 6-1), and follow the directions to initiate the download. It took our laptop about 25 seconds to download the software over a broadband connection.

Figure 6-1

A free download is the first step to making free phone calls.

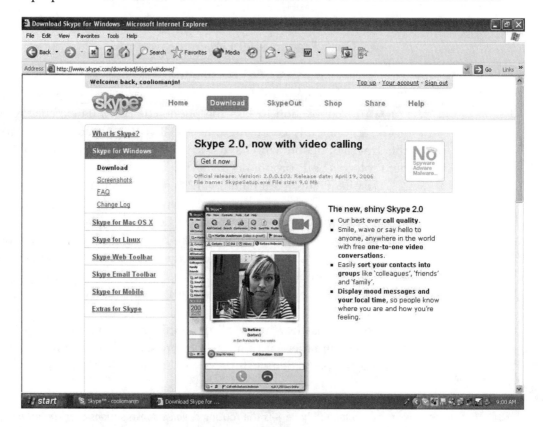

Step 2: Install and Configure Skype

After the download finishes, you should have a blue Skype setup icon on your desktop (or in whichever folder collects your downloads). Click the setup icon and choose your preferred language. After you look over the software license, scratch your head, take a breath—don't worry, we couldn't make heads or tails of it, either—and then click *Accept*. (Rest assured, Skype promises not to sell your name or phone number to other companies or deposit spyware on your computer.) The program will ask you to choose a destination for the software—just click *Next*—and give you a few options about how and when you want Skype to start. Once you're through with that, click *Finish* to launch the software. If you don't already have a Skype account, you'll need to sign up by clicking the link that says *Don't have a Skype name?* Fill in the basic information on the registration pages and the Skype Getting Started wizard will launch (see Figure 6-2). Now, click *Start*. You're about to turn your laptop into a phone.

Figure 6-2

Skype's wizard sets up your laptop for Internet calling.

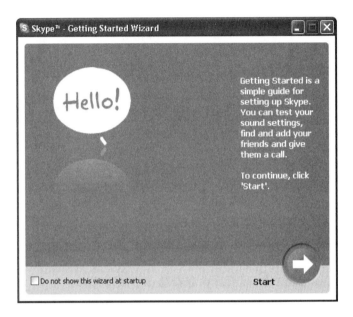

If you've used Skype before, you can skip the wizard, go right to the main interface, and start calling. If you don't want the wizard to start every time you start up Skype, check the Do not show this wizard at startup *box.*

Step 3: Set Off to See the Wizard

Skype's wizard serves two purposes: It gives you a tour of the application and offers a quick way for first-timers to set up an Internet phone. First, the wizard will direct you to make sure that your laptop is online and is equipped with a decent set of speakers and a microphone. Click the green phone icon at the bottom of the Getting Started page of the wizard, and follow the directions (see Figure 6-3). If the audio sounds good, you're ready to move on to Step 4. If it sounds like you're talking through a tin can, you'll need to get a better microphone and/or speakers. Most laptops have speakers built in, and some even have an integrated microphone, though both are usually of less than spectacular quality. We recommend shelling out a few bucks for a USB headset with a built-in microphone and earphones, which will leave your hands free to type or doodle while you yak away.

Figure 6-3

Test your audio quality to make sure it's loud and clear.

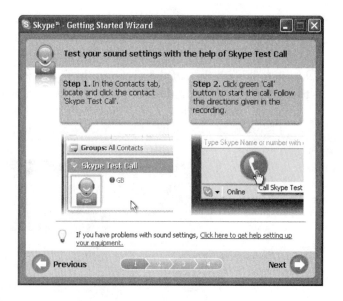

 If you like to walk and talk at the same time, a Bluetooth headset will connect you to your laptop wirelessly from up to 20 feet away. Note that your laptop needs a Bluetooth radio for this to work; if one's not already built in, you can get a Bluetooth PC Card.

Step 4: Add Family and Friends

It's easy to search for and add existing Skype users to your contact list. Just click the *Add Contact* button (see Figure 6-4) and type in a name or e-mail address. If the person is already registered with Skype, they'll show up and with a click of a button you can add them to your address book.

Figure 6-4

Add contacts with the click of a button.

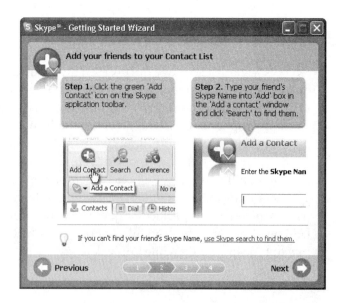

Look Out for Outlook

A nice thing about Skype is that you don't have to enter all of your contacts one by one. Click the *Search* button at the bottom of the wizard's final page, and Skype will launch another wizard to help you import your contacts from

Microsoft Outlook or whichever contact management application you use; unfortunately, you'll still have to hand-type the phone numbers from those paper scraps in your wallet.

Start by clicking on the address book you want to import from and clicking *Next* (see Figure 6-5). You'll probably have to reassure Outlook—a very territorial program—that it's okay to let another program access the contacts. The address book search (see Figure 6-6) should begin.

Unless you have a monstrously large contact list, Skype should be able to get what it needs in 5 minutes or less. But, just to make sure you get everyone, set the Outlook access for 10 minutes.

Figure 6-5

Choose which program you want to import your contacts from.

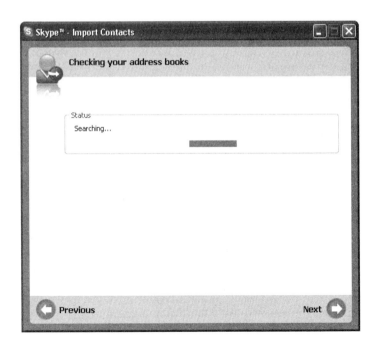

Figure 6-6

Skype will copy the information from your address book into its contact list.

Step 5: Get Ready to Dial

The moment of truth has arrived: It's time to make an Internet phone call. Click on the *Contacts* tab, select the person you want to call, and click the green phone icon at the bottom of the window (see Figure 6-7).

Figure 6-7

Place a call to one of your contacts.

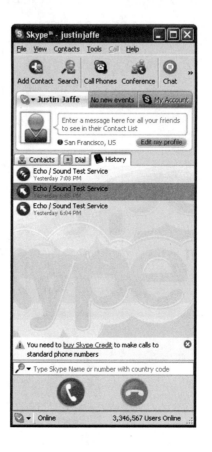

> **tip** *Need to talk to four other people at once? No problem. Click the Conference button, add the other participants, and click Start.*

To call a phone number that's not already in your contact list, click on the *Dial* tab (see Figure 6-8). It'll bring up a keypad, just like the one on a normal phone. Punch in the numbers, and click the green phone icon.

In a couple of seconds, the computer phone you're calling should start ringing. When the person you've called picks up, it should be just like speaking on a normal phone, although audio quality is reliant on the speed of your connection. Note that when someone calls you, you'll click the green phone icon to answer. The red phone icon ends a call.

Figure 6-8

Or make a call using
Skype's dial pad.

SkypeOut and SkypeIn

Skype is terrific for computer-to-computer calling, but you can also call any phone—landline or cell phone—on the planet using the SkypeOut service. It's not free, but unlike a traditional phone service, it doesn't cost much more to call someone who lives halfway across the world than it does to call someone down the block. Most calls cost a penny or two per minute, though dialing up friends in oddball locations (such as the Ascension Islands, for example) will cost a few cents more per minute. To make calls using SkypeOut, you'll need to buy some Skype credits.

Another service, called SkypeIn, lets anyone who isn't using Skype on a computer call you by dialing a regular number—just like a normal phone. What's really cool is that you can choose virtually any phone number, in any area code—if it's not already taken. Compared to most traditional phone service plans, SkypeIn is fairly inexpensive, and comes with a free Skype Voicemail subscription.

Step 6: Set Up Voicemail and Call Forwarding

What phone service would be complete without voicemail? Skype's voicemail service isn't free, but it's fairly inexpensive and easy to set up. You can configure it by clicking on the *Tools* menu, selecting *Options*, and choosing the *Call Forwarding & Voicemail* menu. Take note that your web browser needs to have cookies enabled for it to work. You can record a custom greeting, but be brief, because you have only 5 seconds.

note *Skype transforms your laptop into a fully portable phone. However, for the times you're away from your laptop, you can have your calls forwarded to another computer, landline phone, or cell phone. In the Call Forwarding & Voicemail menu, just type in the phone number you want calls sent to. Note that you need to purchase Skype credit to forward calls to landlines and cell phones.*

Step 7: Add Video to Your Phone Calls

One of the best things about making Internet phone calls is that you can see the people you're calling, and they can see you. That's right—the videophone has arrived. Some laptops have digital video cameras (also called webcams) built-in; if yours doesn't, you'll need to buy one separately. Fortunately, webcams are relatively inexpensive and very easy to set up—just plug the cord into an open USB port and install the included software.

To set up video on Skype, click on the *Tools* menu, select *Options*, and choose the *Video* menu (see Figure 6-9).

Figure 6-9

To set up Skype Video, click here.

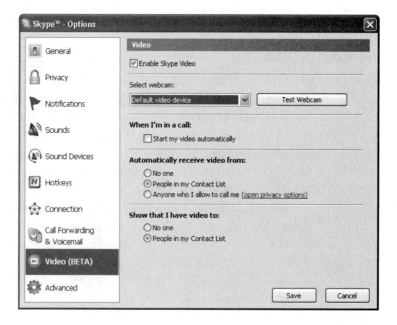

Check the *Enable Skype Video* box, select your webcam, and choose your preferences. The next time you call another Skype user who has a webcam enabled, you'll be able to see them, and they'll see you (see Figure 6-10).

Figure 6-10

Picture this—
a video call.

Transfer an LP or Cassette Tape to CD

What You'll Need:

- Hardware: Record player or other analog audio source; RCA cables, printer (optional)
- Software: Audio Record Wizard; CD-burning software
- Cost: Free to $25 U.S.

Is your closet cluttered with crates of old disco records? Is the back of your car littered with Grateful Dead bootleg tapes? Do you have a complete collection of Chaka Kahn 8-track tapes that's just collecting dust? If you answered yes to any of those questions, we're going to show you how to pull your music collection into the twenty-first century by transferring your old analog recordings—whether they're 45s or 78s, 8-tracks or cassettes, or even reel-to-reel tapes—onto your laptop, where you can store and listen to them or burn them to CD.

The process of moving your older music into the present isn't particularly difficult, though you will need a few modern tools. In addition to a device that will play your source material—a record, tape, or reel-to-reel player—you'll need a little bit of software (and a smidgen of patience). Though your digital recording won't sound as clean or atmospheric as a professionally recorded and engineered CD, it's still worth the effort, especially for homemade recordings or favorite albums that are out of print or just aren't available on CD.

caution *Hmm? Now couldn't you just burn a few more CDs and sell them down there on the corner? Forget about it. Making a copy for yourself is OK, but as soon as you start selling CDs of commercially made records or tapes, you have crossed the line into copyright infringement. Now you're in danger of running afoul of the intellectual property police. Stick to making copies for your own personal use and enjoyment, however, and you're covered under the fair use doctrine of United States copyright law.*

Step 1: Call the Wizard

In Windows, the built-in Sound Recorder software is pitifully rudimentary, and only able to record one minute of audio at a time. If you're going to record Iron Butterfly's *Innagodadavida,* that's not going to cut the mustard. For this project we'll use Audio Record Wizard, available at www.download.com; it's very easy to set up and use, and though the free trial version limits your recordings to an only slightly more palatable maximum of 3 minutes, if you decide that you like it, a reasonable fee will unlock the application and let you record to your heart's content.

  We like Audio Record Wizard, but there plenty of other able recording programs out there. One alternative, NCH Swift Sound's VRS Recording System, is more sophisticated (and more complicated) and includes a CD burner component and audio file editor. You can find it and other digital audio apps at www.download.com.

For now, download Audio Record Wizard, install it, and launch it (see Figure 7-1).

Figure 7-1

The Audio Record Wizard turns any analog audio source into a digital file.

Step 2: Get Connected

Next you need to connect the laptop to whatever source device you'll be recording from—in our case, the record player that's built in to our TEAC SL-A200 mini home stereo (see Figure 7-2). Our stereo has a number of RCA output audio jacks (see Figure 7-3) in the back, and that's what we'll be connecting to. We'll use a cable that has a 3mm audio jack at one end, which we'll plug into the laptop's microphone jack, and a pair of RCA plugs at the other, which will connect to the stereo's RCA jacks.

Figure 7-2

Plug in and fire up
your turntable.

Figure 7-3

The RCA jacks are
located in back.

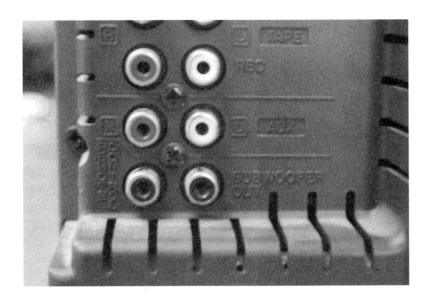

note *If you have a standalone turntable, you can't just connect it directly to the laptop. Most turntables don't produce a strong enough signal for recording. Your record player is probably already hooked up to a stereo receiver or amplifier, so just connect the laptop to the receiver's RCA output jacks. Alternatively, you can get an inexpensive preamp that will do the job.*

Step 3: Get Set to Record

With your connections made, it's time to set up the recording software. Go to the Options menu of Audio Record Wizard, and in the Preferences window, make sure that the recording device is set to Microphone and that the recording volume level is at about one-third of the maximum (see Figure 7-4). Leave the recording quality where it is for now; we'll tweak the settings a bit more later. Right now, we just want to make sure that the signal is getting through.

Figure 7-4

Set the source and the volume.

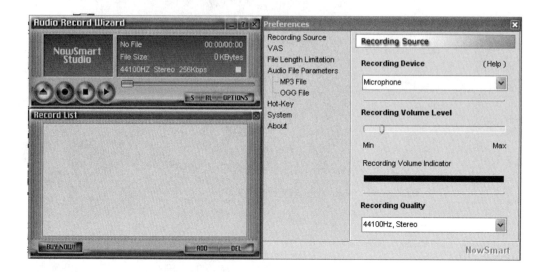

Step 4: Set Your Parameters

Now choose the Audio File Parameters tab from the menu on the left side of the Preferences window. Click on *Audio File Parameters* and click the check box for *Enable Auto-Name System*. Make sure that the *Ext. Name* is set to .mp3; MP3 files take up less disc space than the .wav files that CDs use. (And don't worry—when it comes time to burn a CD, the CD creation software will change it to the right file type.) Now click on the *MP3 File* tab from the left side of the Preferences window (see Figure 7-5); we suggest that you set the *Normal Bitrate* to 256 Kbps, which will provide near-audio-CD quality without taking up an undue amount of hard drive space.

Figure 7-5

Record the file in MP3 format and select your bit rate.

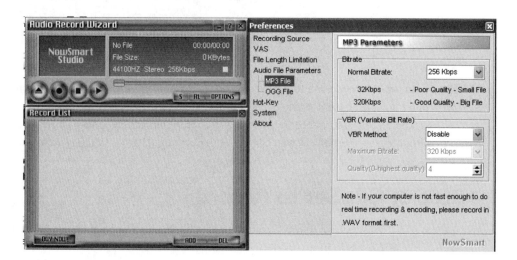

Now that your laptop's pretty much set up, let's make sure your record player is ready to rock. Many turntables have a strobe on the side to calibrate the record's speed; just adjust the speed control knob until the notches on the ring stop moving.

Step 5: Track the Music

Before we go any further, you have a big producer-type decision to make: how to structure your CD. The easiest method is to make a CD with just two tracks on it—one for each side of the record. The downside is that you won't be able to easily skip individual tracks. Alternatively, you can use an audio file editor to break the CD up into a separate track for each tune. It's tedious work and will take a good chunk of extra time, but it'll make your CD a heck of a lot closer to a store-bought disc.

Fortunately, Audio Record Wizard makes it easier to make a track-by-track CD. The software will sequentially name the tracks as you record them; all you have to do is click on the Stop button (yellow with a black square at the center) when a song is over, and then immediately click the Record button (black circle on red background) before the next song starts. You'll have to be quick because there are only a few seconds of dead air between tracks, but it's doable. The software will automatically create a new file for each track, and you can rename the files with the song names later.

Step 6: Test Drive the System

Let's take the whole system for a test drive and create a short recording. Put the needle down anyplace on the record and click Audio Record Wizard's red record button. When the recording starts, you'll see the recording volume indicator start to jump around; adjust the recording volume level so that the end of the bar *just* touches the right side (see Figure 7-6). When you think you've set the level, stop the program—hit the yellow stop button. Now stop the record. To listen to your test track, double-click the file in the *Record List* window. If it sounds good, you're ready. If it sounds distorted or too quiet, adjust the recording volume level accordingly.

Figure 7-6

Set the Recording Volume Level.

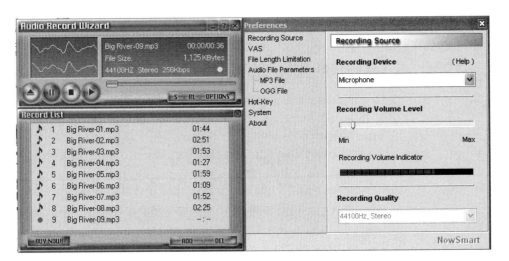

Step 7: Thread the Needle

It's time to make a recording. The timing is a little tricky; unless you happen to have three hands, consider asking a buddy for some help. When you're ready, gently put the needle onto the outer groove of the record (see Figure 7-7) and—quick!—click Audio Record Wizard's red record button.

Figure 7-7

Put the needle on the record.

Step 8: Burn, Baby, Burn

Once your record's tracks have been recorded, it's time to bring them into the future. Right-click on the first track in the Record List and select *Go To the Folder*. The software will automatically open the folder where all of your record's tracks are stored (see Figure 7-8). Just drag them into whichever CD-burning program you're using; and make sure you create an audio CD, as opposed to a data CD or a DVD. Before you burn the disc, double-check that the songs are in the right order. If they aren't, rearrange them.

Step 9: Create a Cover

The final touch is to make a cover for your CD. Nero Burning ROM's Cover Designer is a decent image-editing program that can help you make a jewel case insert that looks nearly professional (see Figure 7-9). We took a digital picture of the record cover, but you could also scan it or find a picture online. Just insert the image into a blank cover and add whatever extra text you want. The program will create a cover that is 4.75 inches by 4.75 inches, so it should just slide into the standard CD jewel case. All you'll have to do is trim away the excess paper.

Figure 7-8

Drag your music into the CD-burning program.

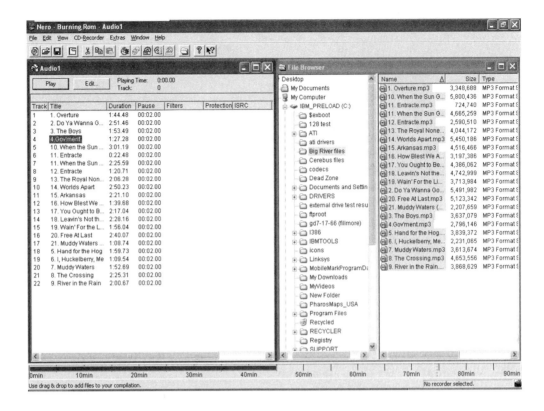

Figure 7-9

Use an image-editing program to trim your cover photo.

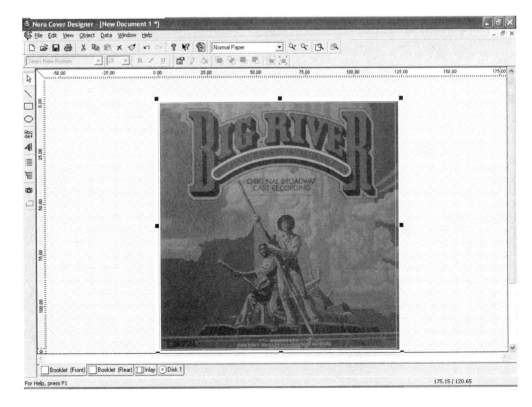

Star in Your Own Internet TV Show

What You'll Need

- Hardware: Webcam
- Software: Webcam software, broadband Internet connection
- Cost: Free to $100 U.S.

One of the coolest and most rewarding ways to waste your time is to turn your laptop into an online TV studio. And with Internet video rapidly gaining ground on the major TV networks, you could be the next superstar of the World Wide Web. All you need is an inexpensive webcam, a broadband Internet connection, and a few good ideas of what people want to watch. (Note: That last element generally separates a popular online program and one that nobody looks at.) Fortunately, public opinion online is amazingly fickle, and a show about your refrigerator, your beer-drinking, or your morning commute all have an equal shot at success (especially if you combine them)—there's simply no accounting for taste in the wild world of webcams.

In fact, two of the most popular webcam shows of all time include a video stream of a coffee pot at MIT and a lobster tank in Maine, so we're not too far out of line by making "Slowy," our 8-year old Golden Greek Tortoise, the star of his own WebTV show. In addition to giving Slowy a shot at the big time, we can keep an eye on him from other parts of the house and when we're on vacation. Everyone wins.

For this project we'll be using Easy Web Cam software, which handles video only—not audio. (It's OK, Slowy's not much of a talker.) There are other programs, however, such as WebCam 1-2-3 and Active WebCam, that let you stream audio and video, which is better for more involved programming like comedy or political punditry, but it requires additional equipment and effort.

Easy Web Cam is available for free at www.download.com. The trial version is fully featured and the company will host your show, but only for 2 weeks; if you become addicted to broadcasting video to the world, pay the nominal license fee and buy it outright. Now, all that's left to say is "Smile, look into the lens, and act naturally."

Step 1: Install the Software

First, you'll need to download the software. Install it and sign off on the program's license agreement by typing "yes" in the box at the lower-left corner (see Figure 8-1).

Figure 8-1

The software license agreement needs to be completed before the TV studio opens.

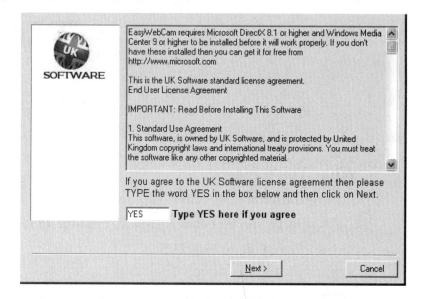

Step 2: Set Your Password

Before you do anything else, you'll have to register your webcam's name and create a password. Easy Web Cam doesn't ask for any personal information beyond your name, interests, and general geographical location. Once you've submitted this info, the company will send you a confirmation e-mail.

tip *For this project, you'll need an Internet connection that's speedy enough to upload images and video streams. Bear in mind that there is broadband and there is broadband, and we're talking about upload speeds here, which vary greatly among cable and DSL providers. We advise a minimum upload speed of about 100 Kbps, but the faster the better. If you're on a dial-up connection, you can still play, but you'll need to reduce your media ambitions: Instead of streaming video, set the software to click a shot every minute or two. Not quite video, but better than nothing.*

Step 3: Try Uploading a Photo

Click on *Capture and Upload* in the main window (see Figure 8-2). The software will attempt to snap a digital photo and upload it to the Web. Let's see if it works.

Figure 8-2

Before trying video, we're starting with a picture.

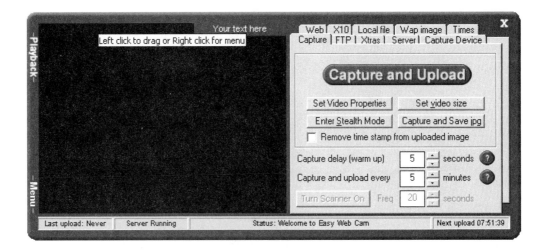

If you're not seeing your webcam's pictures online, click on the FTP tab and make sure that the FTP upload address is **ftp://easyfreewebcam** and that your name and password are correct (see Figure 8-3).

Figure 8-3

Confirm your FTP settings.

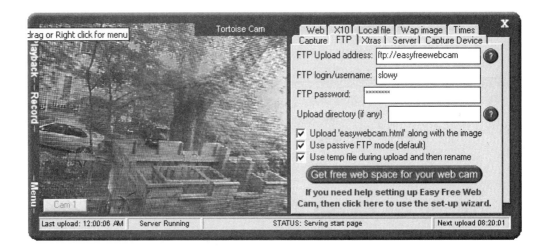

Step 4: Browse Your Cam

At this point your webcam should be online and spewing out digital photos every couple of seconds. In your web browser, go to www.easyfreewebcam.com/cam/[webcam name from Step 2 here] to make sure everything's OK. Is the camera focused? Is it aimed properly? Is the lighting OK? Does the color look right? Slowy's looking good, so we're ready to proceed (see Figure 8-4).

Figure 8-4

Oh, Slowy.

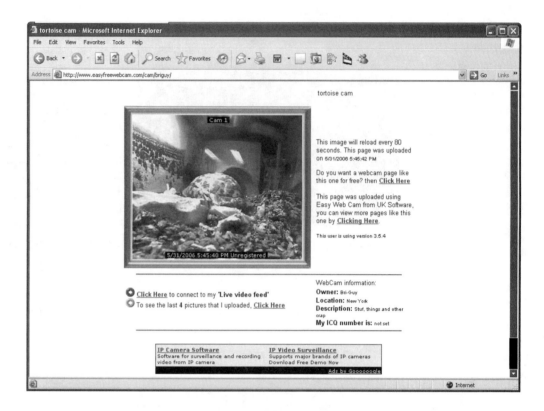

note *If you're not seeing your webcam's pictures online, you may need to initiate a truce between your webcam and your firewall. Disable your firewall briefly to see if the video comes through. If that works, you'll need to configure your firewall so that it knows it's OK to use port 80 for video streaming. Every firewall is different, so look over the manual or Help file for tips on how to do this.*

Step 5: Go to the Video

To start streaming video, click on *Advanced Settings | Server*. Gah! That's a lot of information, but don't be intimidated. This incredibly dense dialog box has controls for just about every detail of webcam operation. We'll explore it further later, but for now, we'll just adjust a few settings.

Uncheck the *Use external IP address* box. Now, check the box for *Enable the built-in web server*. Make sure that the server port is set to 80 (see Figure 8-5).

Figure 8-5

Set the web server
to stream video.

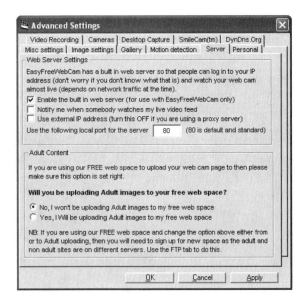

> **tip**   *Planning on doing anything unseemly on camera? (Who are we to judge?) Just make sure you label your webcam show as one that might have risqué content first. Click the Yes check box at the bottom of the Advanced Settings | Server tab. Then, feel free to dance around with your underpants on your head. We sure won't be watching.*

Step 6: Open Your Webcam Page

It's time to try out your webcam. Go back to your browser and refresh the webcam page; you can make sure that it has recently uploaded an image by checking the time stamp at the bottom of the window. You can also click on the yellow circle to see the last few pictures.

Finally, it's the moment we've all been waiting for. Click the red circle to open the video floodgates and allow the streaming to start. After verifying that it's OK to take the risk that the webcam is offline, a new web page should open with your video streaming along (see Figure 8-6).

> **note**   *There's a whole World Wide Web's-worth of cams out there to look at (and laugh at). Go to www.easyfreewebcam.com/LiveWebCams.html to see what's broadcasting live right now. Other webcam pages for perusing the world's video oddballs include www.camscape.com and www.webcamworld.com.*

Step 7: Customize Your Webcam

The good news is that every part of your webcam can be adjusted and customized. The bad news? Every part of your webcam can be adjusted and customized. Fortunately, you can ignore most of the dizzying array of choices. We'll go over a few of the

Figure 8-6

Tortoise cam comes
online. A star is born.

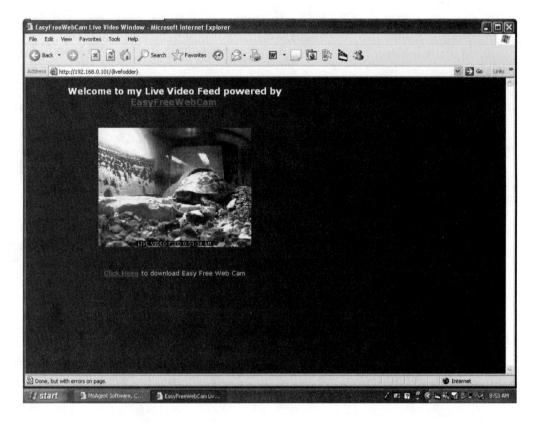

more important ones in the coming steps, but most of this stuff you'll never have to
look at or worry about.

 *The software automatically creates a rather plain-Jane web page for your video stream, but
there are some more lively options available; you can even embed the video player into your own
web page.*

Step 8: Adjust the Resolution

To adjust the video's resolution, click the *Set video size* button in the software's main
window. The Properties dialog box (see Figure 8-7) has a lot going on, but we're most
interested in the output size setting. The higher the output size (also known as the
resolution), the larger and sharper your video window will look in someone's browser, but the less bandwidth you'll have to use for yourself. To keep the video from
eating up all of your bandwidth, we recommend setting the output size to 352 × 288
or lower.

Figure 8-7

Set the video properties
so that the cam doesn't
eat up all your
bandwidth.

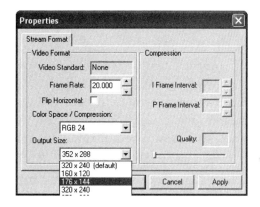

Now, let's look at the frame rate. Normal TV broadcasts about 30 frames per second, but your webcam video should look fine at 10 to 20 frames per second.

Step 9: Allowing Access

One of the fundamental notions of Internet video is that everyone enjoys a bit of voyeurism. But if the thought of your videos reaching far-flung relatives or even the neighbors down the street leaves you shuddering, you can make your Internet video an invitation-only affair. In the Server tab, clicking on the top rectangle opens a dialog box where you can choose who can access the webcam and set individual passwords for them (see Figure 8-8).

Figure 8-8

Keep nosy neighbors
away from your video.

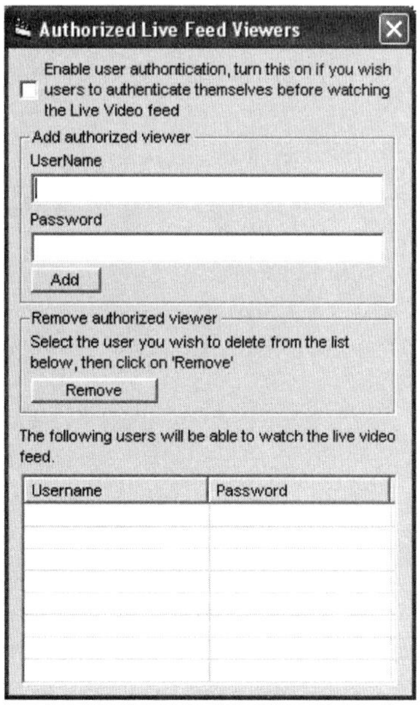

Webcam, Phone Home

If you can't live without checking on your webcam every few minutes, the Easy Web Cam software lets you set up a Wireless Application Protocol (WAP) site to transmit video to your cell phone. The setup isn't simple, and you'll need to work with your service provider to get the right information—where the video should be uploaded, for example—but it's a cool way to take your webcam video with you, wherever you go.

Step 10: Secure the Perimeter

Want to record everything your webcam sees? Want to keep an eye on your front door while you're at work? Go to the Advanced Settings | Video Recording tab (see Figure 8-9). You'll need to select a Codec for encoding the video stream; of the 23 supported by the program, we suggest using Intel's Indeo Video 5.10, which doesn't hog too much of the processor's attention. We recommend that you set the image quality to between 60 and 70. Take note that even at the lowest quality settings, webcam video will eat up your hard drive faster than you can say "Action"; so that you don't wind up with 8 hours of nothing, select the *When motion is detected* check box, and the webcam will only record when something interesting happens.

Figure 8-9

Turn your webcam into a surveillance camera.

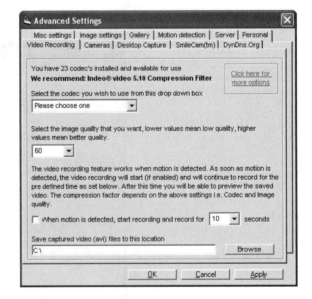

Step 11: Hit the Road

The reason you got a laptop was so you could take it anywhere; the great thing is that now your webcam can go along for the ride. To keep your video broadcasting, you'll need to stay close to a WiFi network; alternatively, you can use a cell network data card and account to create a mobile webcam studio that can document a trip to the beach or just your daily commute.

tip *If your video freezes up on you, try refreshing your browser a few times. If that doesn't help, increase the amount of cache your browser can use to hold at least 10 GB. If you're using Internet Explorer, go to Tools | Internet Options | Temporary Internet files, and use the slider to set the cache amount.*

Broadcast a Podcast

What You'll Need

- Hardware: Microphone, headphones, broadband Internet connection
- Software: ePodcast Creator (Audio Software)
- Cost: Free to $150 U.S.

Andy Warhol once said, "In the future everyone will be famous for 15 minutes." Well, Andy, the future is now. With the rise of the Internet, new media have proliferated to the point where anyone with a computer, a microphone, and a broadband connection—namely, you—can broadcast themselves to every corner of the earth. Warhol also said, "In 15 minutes everybody will be famous." Well, guess what? It's your turn.

Podcasting is a method of distributing multimedia files, most often radio-style programs or music videos, over the Internet for playback on mobile devices and personal computers. It's not called a podcast for nothing; the iPod has become so popular that it's become synonymous with portable digital audio players. Podcasts don't discriminate, however, and can be played on any digital music player as well as any desktop PC or laptop. As popular as podcasting has become, it stops short of letting you create a live Internet radio station because everything is in a premade, self-contained audio file. Still, it's a good way to sound off on whatever you want.

For this audio-intensive project we'll be putting together a bluegrass radio show using Industrial Audio Software's ePodcast Creator, a simple but powerful application that walks you through the process. The 30-day trial is free but includes an annoying advertisement. (A simpler version, ePodcast Express, and a professional version, called ePodcast Producer, are also available). As usual, you can find dozens of alternatives at www.download.com.

Do Your Homework

Podcasting is like beer—you can't be sure what you like until you try everything, so get ready for a bender. From weekly updates on European football to poetry to the latest research in dermatology, we suggest you do a little research on the competition before you get started. Here are a few good places to check out:

- www.Podcast.net
- www.Podcastalley.com
- www.apple.com/itunes/Podcast
- www.Podcastingnews.com
- www.podcasts.yahoo.com

Step 1: Get Activated

After downloading and installing the software, you'll have to fill out a form with your name and e-mail address. You'll soon get an e-mail with a code that will open the program. Enter the code in the Enter Activation Key box (see Figure 9-1).

Figure 9-1

Type in your key
to get started.

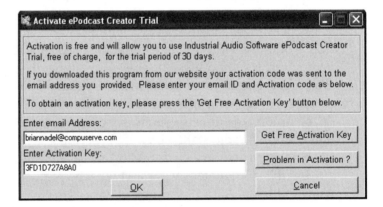

Step 2: Pick a Task, Any Task

The ePodcast Creator program starts by asking you whether you want to open a pre-existing podcast or a new one. Call us crazy, but we're going to begin by selecting *New Podcast* (see Figure 9-2). If you want to bypass this opening screen in the future, click the check box in the lower-left corner.

Figure 9-2

Start anew.

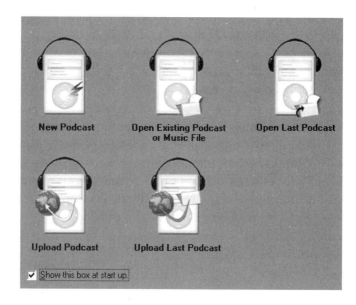

New Podcast   Open Existing Podcast   Open Last Podcast
              or Music File

Upload Podcast   Upload Last Podcast

☑ Show this box at start up.

Step 3: Choose Quantity or Quality

Next you must decide what level of audio quality you want your podcast to be. The choices are fairly self-explanatory: CD quality will deliver the crispest, clearest audio, while AM radio is on the rough side. Because we've long fantasized about being a disk jockey, we're going to go mid-range and podcast in FM quality (see Figure 9-3); we'll still get stereo sound, but at half the sampling rate of CD quality.

 Higher audio quality may sound better to the listener but will result in a larger file (and a longer download for your listeners). We recommend that you pick a comfortable spot in the middle. Don't worry; you're not married to the format, because you can do your next installment at any quality level you want.

Figure 9-3

AM, FM, or CD quality, your choice.

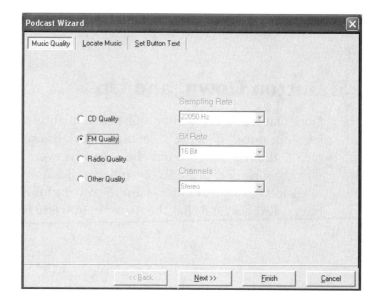

Most computers have crappy sound capabilities, so most people won't be able to hear the difference between a great audio file and a mediocre one, anyway.

Step 4: Find Your Music

Next click the Locate Music tab, show the program where you keep your music (Figure 9-4), and select the tracks you want to play. (You can pick tunes from different locations on your laptop, but it make things easier if all of your music resides in one folder.) Of course, you don't have to choose music; any kind of audio file or snippet will come in handy for a podcast. You can use recorded interviews, sound effects, or anything that a microphone can pick up.

Figure 9-4

Show ePodcast Creator where you keep your music.

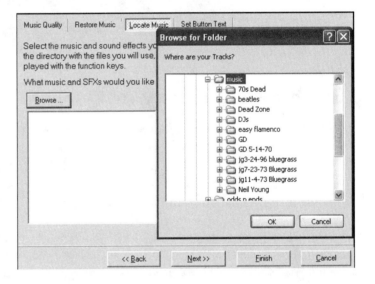

note *Sound effects can transform a basic podcast into a radio-broadcast-caliber show. We recommend nosing around the Web for one of the many free sound effects sites or hitting an online music store and picking up a CD's-worth of sound effects.*

Step 5: Button Down, and Up

Now that we've decided on our music quality and shown the program where we keep our music, it's time to set button text. Basically, you'll be assigning a button to each audio file (song, sound effect, or whatever) you plan to use; when it's time to play the song or sound effect, you'll just click its button.

Select a song that you'll want to play during the podcast, type its name into the Button Text box, and click the *Assign* button (see Figure 9-5).

Figure 9-5

Assigning buttons to
your tracks makes
podcasting easy.

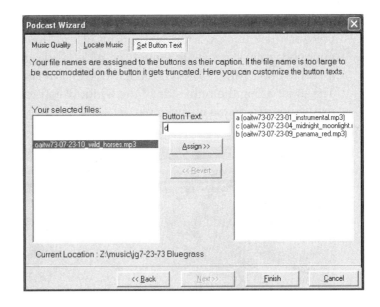

If you neglect to assign your songs, the program will automatically create buttons
for the first 12 of them. Once you're done assigning the songs, the software will take
a minute to prepare your audio tracks and buttons (see Figure 9-6).

Figure 9-6

Time to make
the buttons.

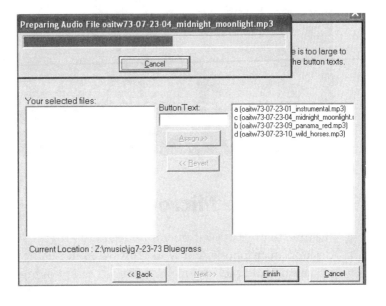

tip   *Although you can choose to click the buttons in any order, it'll make things simpler if you assign
and create them in the order you plan to play them.*

Step 6: Make Yourself at Home

The ePodcast control panel puts everything you'll need for your show at your fingertips. The two rectangular boxes in the middle are where music and vocals are tracked;
the playback and recording control panels sit along the left side, complete with start

and stop buttons, a digital timer, and volume control sliders (see Figure 9-7). To save a voice or music track, use the oval buttons placed along the top of the window. To record your podcast in stereo, with roughly equal left and right levels—which we recommend, if you're pod casting solo—click the *Lock L/R Volumes* button in the upper-right corner. The slider along the right side of the window controls the voice and music mix; we'll use it later to fade the music in while fading out the microphone and vice versa.

Figure 9-7

Your podcasting control panel.

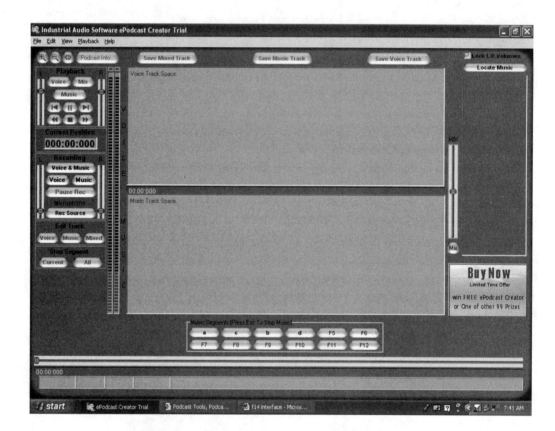

Step 7: Plug in the Microphone

It's time to plug in your microphone and warm up your vocal chords. An old-school, desktop microphone will work, but we prefer using a headset with a built-in microphone to avoid picking up stray sounds or annoying echoes.

Step 8: Create Your First Podcast

Let's get this podcast on the road. Following the conventional radio show format, we're going to play some opening music, talk for a spell, spin a few tunes, and wrap things up.

On the Recording panel, click the *Rec Source* button a few times until it displays the correct input for the microphone. (You can also select other inputs, such as a CD or cassette-tape player). Now click the button you assigned to your opening music track (see Figure 9-8). Once the music has started, click the *Voice & Music* button. Slowly nudge the mix slider up (into the Voice area) and introduce your show. The further the slider goes into voice territory, the louder your voice and the softer the music. Talk over the music for a few seconds, and then gradually shift to voice only. It's a lot to concentrate on; consider enlisting a friend to act as the show's engineer and handle the controls.

Step 9: Play That Funky Music

When you're done with your intro, click the button you assigned to a music track, and click the mix slider back down to the music section. Try to get the sound levels so they just touch the top of the bar—it'll take a little bit of juggling to get it just right for each track.

All the while, the Recording box will be blinking red, indicating that it's taping; the timer will keep track of how long your show is.

Figure 9-8

Punch in your intro music, and start talking.

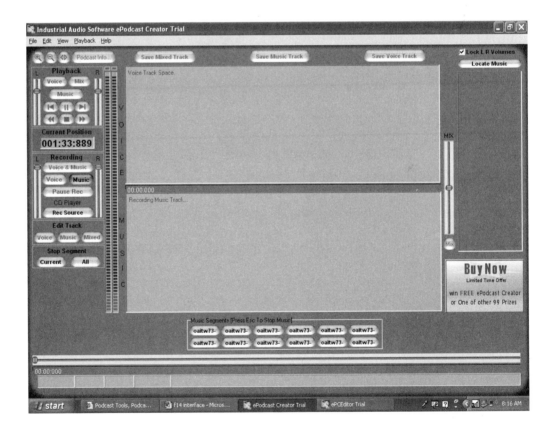

tip
Be aware when you're recording; a good microphone will pick up everything from heavy breathing to digestive noises to the phone ringing in the next room. Of course, that's not necessarily a bad thing. We recommend setting up your studio in a room with decent acoustics, even a closet.

Step 10: Wrap It Up

As the music track ends, we'll move the mix slider upward again and start talking. It takes a bit of coordination to do this without babbling or freezing up, so a few practice runs might be called for. After you've wrapped up the show and signed off, click the *Stop Segment | All* button.

The program will display the rough cut of your podcast (see Figure 9-9). The squiggly lines represent the audio levels for your voice (top window) and the music (bottom window). To review your show, click the *Playback | Mix* button. Was your mixing smooth? Did you pick up unwanted extraneous noises, such as the air conditioner or the TV? Did you say anything untoward? If so, don't worry—it's not as if you were paying for studio time. Record a second take.

Figure 9-9

Preview your podcast.

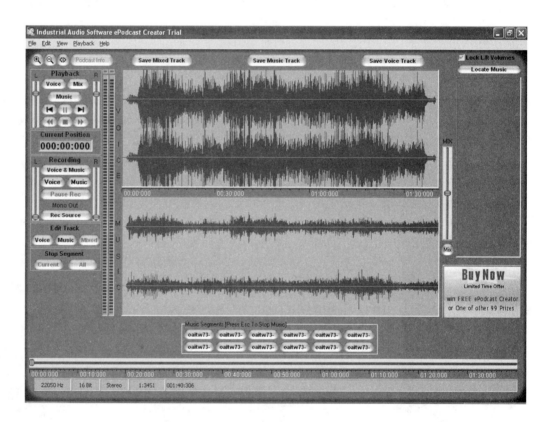

tip   *The program comes with a competent audio editor, which lets you tweak and adjust the levels. Post production cleanup can elevate your podcast to the next level. Don't be afraid to experiment.*

Step 11: Save Yourself

You've recorded your show and are happy with the result. Save the file with a descriptive title (sorry, no spaces in the file name); the program will automatically save it as an MP3. Now you need to upload it to a server so the world can access it.

note *To publicize your podcast and let listeners know when you've released a new show, you'll be taking advantage of RSS, which stands for Really Simple Syndication or Rich Site Summary, depending on who you ask. RSS is a kind of web feed that automatically notifies your listeners when you've released a new podcast episode. Your upload server will take care of this automatically.*

Step 12: Get Set to Upload

Click on *File | Upload Podcast*. Now fill in the server name and address—information that will come from the site that's hosting your show (see Figure 9-10).

Figure 9-10

From your laptop to the world, via FTP.

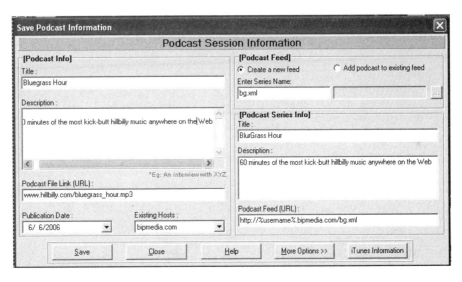

tip *If you plan to start an ongoing series, say a daily or weekly show, select the* Add podcast to existing feed *option; that way, your shows will be listed together, in order.*

DJ a Party

What You'll Need

- Hardware: Powered speakers (optional), Xitel Pro HiFi Link (optional), microphone (optional)
- Software: AtomixMP3 Virtual DJ, Music Morpher
- Cost: Free to $150 U.S.

Whether you're using vinyl LPs or CDs, a traditional DJ setup can quickly run into the hundreds—if not thousands—of dollars. You need turntables, a mixer, amps and speakers, lots of heavy-duty cables, not to mention crates and crates of records or CDs. The only thing worse than paying for all this equipment is hauling it around from gig to gig.

Amazingly, you can rock a party just as hard with a laptop, a few pieces of software (that are free to try), and a few megabytes of digital music. And if you're playing to a crowd of two or more, you'll definitely need a louder pair of speakers than the ones built into your laptop. While being a party DJ sounds complicated and technically involved, if you already have a decent collection of music on your laptop, you're more than halfway there.

In this chapter we'll show you how to get started with the basics: mixing tracks, adding effects, making karaoke tracks, and even scratching. We'll be using two programs, Virtual DJ and Music Morpher, and only scratching the surface of all that they can do.

Anyone with lots of MP3s and a smidgeon of musical ability can become a convincing laptop DJ. The bling, posse, and bodyguards are purely optional.

Step 1: Choose Your Name

First things first: pick your DJ name. (Remember, be humble: You're probably not the Grand Master of anything quite yet.)

Step 2: Download Your Turntables

Now, download the AtomixMP3 Virtual DJ software at www.download.com. (Take note that the trial version lasts for only 20 days.) Once it's downloaded, install it, and launch it.

Step 3: Dig Through the Crates

Before the Virtual DJ starts, it will ask you to let it check for any updates that AtomixMP3 might have made; let it do so. The software will then automatically scan your hard drive for digital music to create a database of tunes (see Figure 10-1).

Figure 10-1

Virtual DJ searches your hard drive for music.

Step 4: Let the Record Play

Once the program has discovered your cache of music (if you have one), the MP3s will appear in the playlist window below the decks. Just drag a file onto one of the decks and click the Play button to start it. While it gets going, drag another song onto the other deck.

Step 5: Get Faded

Now here's the tricky part: as the first song ends on deck 1, click *Play* on deck 2 and start sliding the *crossfader* (see Figure 10-2) to gradually mix in the new song.

The quicker you move the fader, the sharper the transition. You can move the fader back and forth quickly to tease in the new song, or gradually to make a subtle, smooth transition. Now, as the song on deck 2 starts to play, go ahead and load up the next tune on deck 1.

Don't look now, but you just became a DJ.

Figure 10-2

Slide the crossfade bar back and forth to mix.

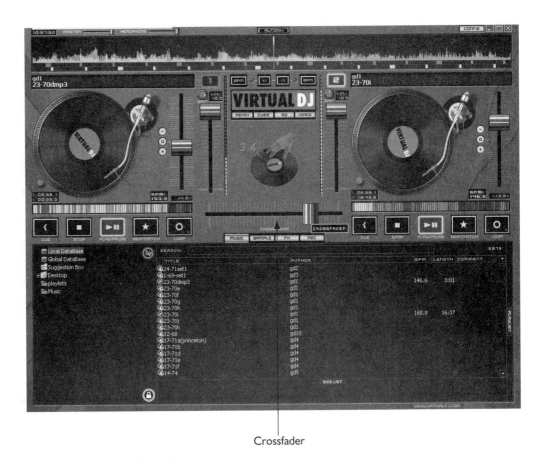

Crossfader

Step 6: Catch the Pitch

Now, it's time to get a little fancy. You can adjust the speed of each song by moving the pitch control (see Figure 10-3), located just to the right of each deck, up (to slow it down) or down (to speed it up).

Step 7: Get On Beat

One of the reasons we like Virtual DJ is that it makes mixing easy. The software's Beat-Match function protects you from making embarrassing mixing messes; it makes sure that the tunes on the two turntables are in synch by slowing down the faster track and speeding up the slower one. With songs playing on each deck, click the *BeatMatch* button on each deck to synch up the beats.

tip *BeatMatch doesn't always deliver the results you're looking for. You can set the beats per minute (BPM) manually, however, by working the pitch control slider or clicking the plus and minus buttons directly to the right of each deck.*

Figure 10-3

The pitch control speeds up or slows down a track.

Pitch control sliders

Step 8: Find or Make Samples

The next bag of tricks comes from clicking the *Sample* button below the crossfader, which will bring up a small library of prerecorded samples (see Figure 10-4), including a siren, a saxophone jingle, and some debatable club chants.

Even better, you can record your own samples and use them to punctuate your live performances—or loop them up to create your own miniature tracks. Just click the *Loop* button below the volume slider and Virtual DJ will capture a few seconds whatever song is playing, loop it up, and replay it.

Step 9: Create FX Effects

In addition to simple samples and loops, Virtual DJ offers some more advanced effects. Click on the *FX* button below the crossfader to bring up a rack of preloaded effects (see Figure 10-5); many more are available for download on the AtomixMP3 web site. The effects are simple to use—just drag one of them into the channel 1 column (to manipulate the sound on deck 1) or channel 2 (to mess with the audio on deck 2); you can use up to three effects—separately or simultaneously—for each turntable.

Figure 10-4

Sample the
samples.

Figure 10-5

Add some flavor
with sound effects.

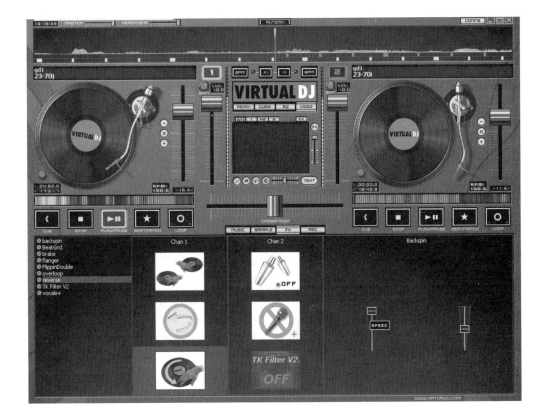

Step 10: Step It Up

OK, you've got the basics down. And that's just enough to convincingly DJ a party.

But now we'll press on a little further and show you how to manipulate existing tracks and make your own. Our preferred tool is Music Morpher, a free download that lets you create remixes, splice tracks and audio clips, make your own karaoke tracks, and enhance tracks with audio effects. Go ahead and download it from www. musicmorpher.com, install it, and open it.

Step 11: Get Oriented

The top pane lets you navigate around your laptop to select and load music files; the one on the right is for adding sound effects; and the bottom area lets you adjust the pitch and timbre of any given track (see Figure 10-6).

There are even player controls and a graphic equalizer in the lower right for fine-tuning. Need a little more treble? Push the bars on the right up. More bass? Try the ones at the left.

Figure 10-6

Music Morpher's controls sit front and center.

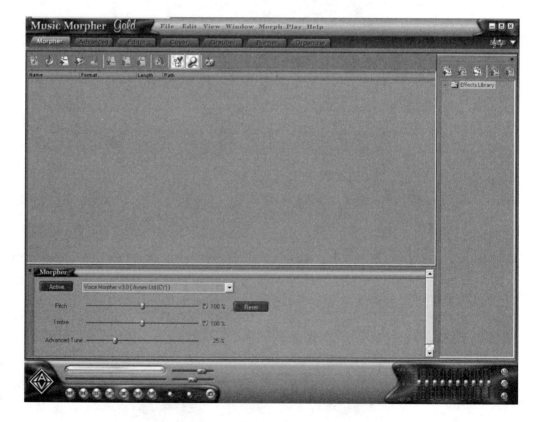

Step 12: Build a Playlist

Use the file open icon in the upper-left corner to put some tunes into the Morpher's main window. It'll show the type of file, the length, and the source (see Figure 10-7). Before you do anything else, save it as a *Playlist*, the digital equivalent of a mix tape.

Figure 10-7

String some tracks together.

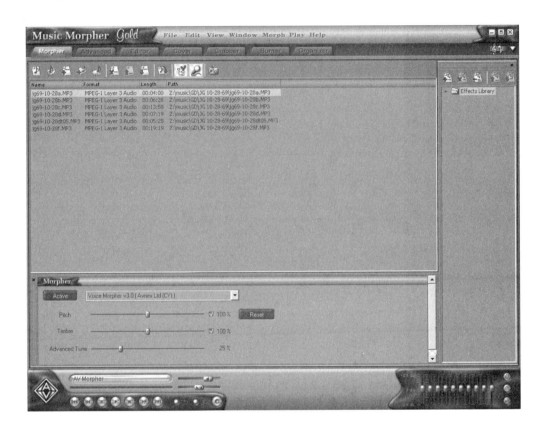

If you don't have much music already loaded onto your laptop, you can download songs from a variety of online music stores. MP3.com lets you shop from a number of music stores at once.

Step 13: Clean It Up

If you're playing tracks you recorded from an LP or cassette (the subject of Chapter 7), Music Morpher can help you improve the sound. Click the *Advanced* tab at the top, and drag the track you want to work on into the window.

Next, click the icon that looks like a speaker and a plus symbol in the Effects window. Select *New complex* (see Figure 10-8); when an empty *New complex* file shows up at the bottom of the file list, right-click on it and select *Add New SubEffect*, which will bring up a seemingly endless list of available effects. Click on *Noise reduction* to get rid of static or feedback.

Figure 10-8

Get rid of the static.

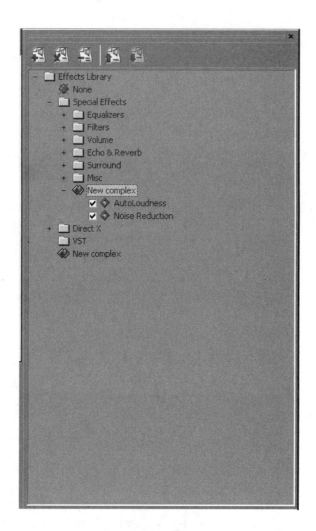

Step 14: Say Ho!

If you're the type of DJ who's not content to just spin tunes, but wants to chant, rap, or sing along, plug in that microphone and let's get busy.

Step 15: Use Karaoke

It's pretty easy to delete the vocals from a song. First, go to the *Editor* tab and open a song. Once the song loads, the software will display a graph of the song's various audio levels. Next, go into the *Effects Library*, select the Karaoke effect, and let the software do its thing. It may not be perfect, but it'll be good enough to let someone else shine on the vocal parts.

tip *Use the Voice Extractor effect to isolate the vocal track from the background music; it's a useful tool for creating your own a cappella tracks for remixes.*

Upgrade Your Sound

Though your laptop's sound quality might be adequate for casual headphone listening, it's not good enough to rock a party at high volume. You can turn your laptop into a performance-caliber tool with Xitel's Pro HiFi Link (Figure 10-9), which redirects the audio signal from your laptop's cheesy sound card and speakers to a small box via USB. In addition to improving the audio sound quality, the box has jacks for coaxial, RCA, and even optical audio connections to connect to your home stereo or a pair of pro speakers. Even better, the HiFi Link comes with professional-grade audio cables.

Figure 10-9

Turn your laptop into a party-caliber music machine.

Part II

Challenging

Watch and Record TV

What You'll Need

- Hardware: TV Tuner (USB or PC Card)
- Software: Included
- Cost: $75 U.S.

Prediction: In the not-so-distant future, computers and televisions will merge into one super-media device, on which you'll be able to surf the web, send e-mail, play games, and even get work done—all while watching your favorite TV show. Good news: the not-so-distant-future is about a half-hour from now. While only the most expensive, tricked-out models come already equipped with TV functionality, it's really not all that hard to make your own laptop TV. All you need is a basic TV tuner that connects to your laptop via a USB 2.0 port or plugs directly into your laptop's PC Card slot.

Laptop TV has some great advantages over traditional TV: unlike your digital cable's scrolling program guide or even—yechh—the old-school one printed in the Sunday newspaper, most laptop TV tuners come with an interactive, online electronic program guide (EPG) that not only tells you what shows are on, but includes an episode summary, and provides details about the actors in each episode or movie. Even better, recording TV shows and movies is as easy as the push of a button, and from there it's a snap to burn your shows onto DVD. (Of course, if you don't want to bother with burning DVDs, you can always store programs on your hard drive, though you'll need a big one; video eats up hard drive space fairly quickly.) And best of all, a TV tuner will transform your laptop into a personal video recorder—à la Tivo—that will let you pause and rewind live TV, make it easy to schedule the recording all of your favorite shows, and keep your recorded shows organized and easily accessible.

Though there are a number of great TV tuners on the market, we'll use ATI's TV Wonder USB 2.0 tuner, to demonstrate (see Figure 11-1).

Figure 11-1

ATI's TV Wonder TV
tuner connects via USB.

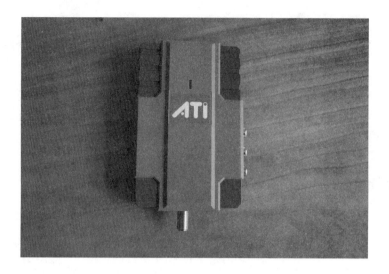

Step 1: Install the Software

Before you can actually connect your TV tuner to your laptop, you'll need to load
the software from the included CD. Once that's done, go to ATI's web site (www.ati
.com), and check in the "Drivers & Software" section to see if there are any patches or
updates for the software. Also, because many tuner programs use Windows Media
Player, make sure you have the latest updates for Windows. There's a lot of software
to install, but it should progress automatically. Be prepared to restart your laptop at
least once.

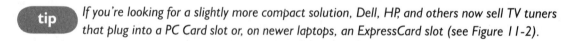 *If you're looking for a slightly more compact solution, Dell, HP, and others now sell TV tuners
that plug into a PC Card slot or, on newer laptops, an ExpressCard slot (see Figure 11-2).*

Figure 11-2

HP's ExpressCard
TV tuner.

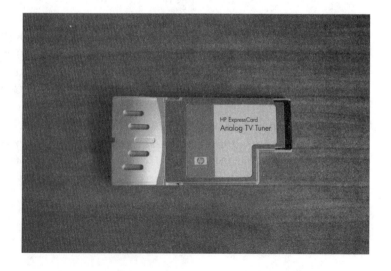

Step 2: Plug In

A few minutes into the software setup, the program will prompt you to plug in the USB tuner. You'll connect it to your laptop via an open USB 2.0 port and then plug your TV cable or antenna directly into the tuner's coaxial port (see Figure 11-3). Finally, you'll have to use the AC adapter to power the device.

Figure 11-3

Plug in the antenna or cable line, power, and USB line when the software asks for it.

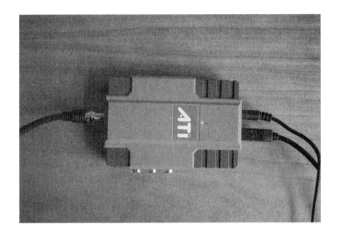

note   *In addition to adding TV reception to your laptop, most TV tuners also accept signals from a variety of other sources, such as a DVD player, Tivo, or camcorder. With the ATI TV tuner, your laptop can connect to virtually any audio/visual component that has an S-video or Composite video input or stereo RCA audio jacks (see Figure 11-4).*

Figure 11-4

Adding multiple connections to your laptop.

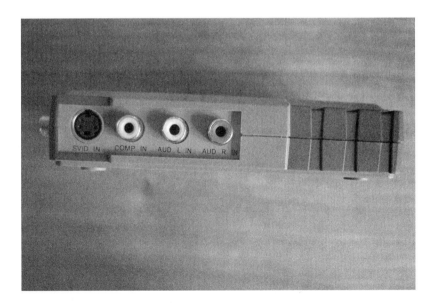

Step 3: Follow the TV Wizard

OK, now that the software's installed and all of the connections have been made, start up the ATI's Multimedia Center software. Before you can get started, you'll need to agree to the incomprehensible software license; once you've accepted the terms, the TV Initialization Wizard will start up (see Figure 11-5).

Figure 11-5

The wizard starts turning your notebook into a TV.

The wizard will ask you some personal questions—where you live, what type of TV connection you're using—so that it can set up the correct TV format and locate your cable provider, if necessary. Once you've told the wizard whether the TV tuner is connected to an antenna or cable, click *Autoscan* (see Figure 11-6). At this point, the software will search for all available channels, which should take about a minute or so.

Figure 11-6

Enter where you live and Autoscan looks for available channels.

Step 4: Beware of Children

Now that your TV is set up and working, you can establish a password that can block certain channels and settings. We're pretty sure that TV programming is guaranteed to all citizens—maybe somewhere in the Bill of Rights?—but if you regularly come into contact with small, unruly TV-obsessed children, go ahead and set a password (see Figure 11-7).

Figure 11-7

A password can keep homework time sacred.

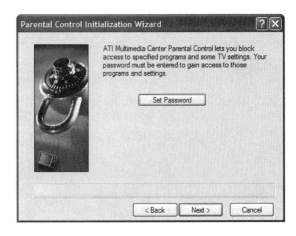

Step 5: Set Some More Settings

Next the software will ask which format you want your digital TV broadcast in (see Figure 11-8). We prefer MPEG-2 because it contains more information than the highly compressed MPEG-4 format and it's the easiest format for burning shows onto DVD. MPEG-2 files take up more disk space than ATI's VCR format, however, and the Windows Media Format is the best for streaming over a network.

Figure 11-8

Pick a format— any format.

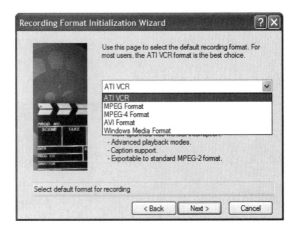

note *MPEG-2 and MPEG-4 are the designation for a group of coding and compression standards for audio and video, as agreed upon by the Moving Pictures Experts Group. MPEG-2 is typically used to encode DVDs, audio, and video for broadcast signals, including direct broadcast satellite and cable TV, and with some modifications, is also the coding format used by standard commercial DVD movies. MPEG-4 is used for video transmission over the web and to mobile devices such as cell phones.*

Step 6: Store Your TV Shows

Now you need to set aside some free space on your laptop's hard drive to store your TV shows. Because we intend to either delete shows right after we watch them (or move them straight onto DVDs, if we want to keep them), we're going to cordon off only 10 GB for our digital recordings (see Figure 11-9). OK, 10 GB is a pretty good amount of space, but MPEG-2 files take up about one megabyte per second of TV time. (Ten gigs will give us about three hours of TV—about enough for a couple of shows plus a movie.) If you're running low on space, you may need to go get an external hard drive; and take note, due to the bandwidth and instant response required, network hard drives won't cut the mustard.

Figure 11-9

Set aside disk space for TV recordings.

tip *If you're feeling advanced, the Advanced Settings button will bring you into the TV-on-Demand Advanced Settings dialog box, in which you can control and fine-tune the processor load, image quality, and video performance parameters (see Figure 11-10). Be careful; if you select High CPU Load, or turn some of the other settings up too high, the program will bog your laptop down when recording video.*

Figure 11-10

Set video recording parameters.

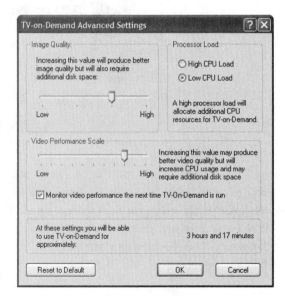

Step 7: Try Out Your New Tube

It's the moment of truth: you can now watch TV right on your laptop. In fact, after you click *Finish*, you should see live TV on the screen, so sit back and enjoy the view (see Figure 11-11).

Figure 11-11

You're ready to watch TV.

tip   *To resize the TV window, you can grab a corner, left-click, and drag it to the right size. You can also use the CTRL key to change the window's resolution:*

- CTRL-1: 160×120
- CTRL-2: 240×180
- CTRL-3: 640×480

Step 8: Surf Channels

Unlike with your television, you can adjust and control just about everything—from volume to brightness to the size of the picture—on your laptop TV. With the ATI player, the oval-shaped menu includes buttons for changing channels, initiating recording, taking a screen capture, adding closed captions, muting the sound, and more. You can change the channel directly with the up and down arrows or number keys (see Figure 11-12).

Figure 11-12

Your own software
remote control.

tip   *One of the coolest things your laptop TV can do is display multiple channels simultaneously, which
can be especially hypnotic late at night when nothing worth watching is actually on. It's like having dozens of tiny TVs lined up for your perusal. Click the Channel Surf button (the little eye icon)
and you'll see a screen full of tiny images of every show that's currently available. It can show
nearly 90 channels at once, which update every few seconds. Select any show by clicking on it.*

Step 9: Set Even More Settings

Toward the bottom of the player is a little box with the check in it. Clicking this icon
will bring up the TV Setup dialog box. There are a lot of settings, and most will never
need to be fiddled with (see Figure 11-13).

Figure 11-13

Control the TV screen
basics.

If you're going to spend any time in this menu, we recommend adjusting the screen
brightness and color balance to optimize the quality of the TV picture (see Figure 11-14).
Also worth double-checking are the closed-caption options.

Figure 11-14

Brightness, color, tint—it's all at your fingertips.

> **tip** One neat trick is to set the TV window as your computer's desktop. Whatever's on, commercials and all, will remain front and center; just make sure to clear out all of the desktop icons. Trust us: This will impress your friends. Press the Function 7 (F7) key to turn it on.

Step 10: Throw Out Your TV Guide

Most TV tuners, including the ATI's TV Wonder, come with an electronic program guide. The ATI TV tuner comes with Gemstar's guide (see Figure 11-15). Click the *Guide Plus+* icon to configure and open the programming guide; you'll be required to register first.

> **tip** Though there are many good guides out there, we also like the Zap2it guide, available online at www.zap2it.com.

Step 11: Get the Details

When you see something you like in the program guide, double-click the listing and you'll get all the details—a summary of the episode, the rating, even which actors are in it (see Figure 11-16). Also displayed are listings for when other shows in the series are scheduled to be shown.

Figure 11-15

Find out what's on with the programming guide.

Figure 11-16

The gritty details of every show on TV.

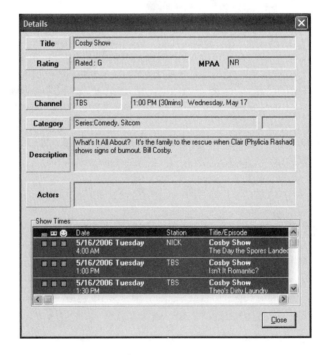

Every two weeks or so, the EPG will warn you that your listings are out of date and need freshening up. Updates are free, but the EPG will not automatically refresh itself, unfortunately.

Step 12: Record It, Now or Later

It's absurdly easy to set the software to tape any and all of the shows you want in the program guide (it's *so* much easier than setting up that old VCR). Just right-click on any show in the guide, click *Record,* and the software will take care of the rest (see Figure 11-17).

Figure 11-17

Right-click on any listing to immediately watch, record, or set it as a favorite.

Your recordings will end up in the ATI Media Library folder, from which you can play them, delete them, or burn them onto DVDs.

You can also record whatever show you're watching, spur of the moment, by clicking on the small camera icon in center of the player panel. Because the ATI TV Wonder is a single-tuner device, you can only watch one show at a time and you can't record one show while watching another. There are, however, more expensive dual-tuner devices that can.

Step 13: Get Back On the Couch

What TV would be complete without a remote control? Most TV tuners come with a handheld remote control, including the ATI TV Wonder, though other companies sell the remote separately (see Figure 11-18).

Figure 11-18

Do it all, right from the couch.

Plug the remote's receiver into an open USB slot, and let the software install itself. If it software doesn't install itself automatically, you may need to go to ATI's web site, download the remote program, and install it. The remote can not only control the channels, adjust the volume, and initiate and stop recording, but it can also control the mouse and shut the laptop off from afar.

Transfer Home Video to DVD

What You'll Need

- Hardware: Camcorder, cables, DVD (or CD) burner
- Software: Microsoft Movie Maker
- Cost: Free to $100 U.S.

L ike most people, we have piles of videotapes chronicling our lives, from birthday parties to high school graduations to weddings. Every once in a while, we hook our camera up to the TV, haphazardly search for an interesting clip to watch, and bore the pants off our relatives. Sound familiar?

In this chapter, we're going to show you how to take a plain old home movie and spice it up by adding some Hollywood-style editing, transitions, titles, and special effects. And when we're done, we'll burn it on to a DVD, for a professional-looking product.

caution *Whether they use flash cards, optical discs, or Mini DV tapes, most modern camcorders record video digitally, which makes it fairly easy to put the footage right onto a laptop hard drive. If you've got an older analog video camera that uses VHS (or—gasp!—Betamax) tapes, you'll need a digitizer to help you import your video from your camera to your laptop. Digitizers are available from companies such as Pinnacle Systems and Sonic Solutions.*

Our video-editing software of choice is Microsoft Movie Maker, included with recent versions of Windows and available for free download. Though it's not the simplest or most powerful program, Movie Maker lets you capture video clips, storyboard them, and add professional effects and cinematic transitions. And when you're done, it's a snap to burn it onto a DVD.

Step 1: Shake Your Movie Maker

If your laptop runs Windows XP, it probably already has the Movie Maker software on it; to check, go to Start | All Programs | Accessories. If you don't have Movie Maker, download it for free from Microsoft's web site, install it, and launch it.

Step 2: Get Connected

Next, connect your video camera to your to laptop with a USB or FireWire cable (see Figure 12-1). Make sure the camera's AC adapter is plugged in (we don't want it running out of battery power in the middle of our session), and turn it on.

Figure 12-1

Connect the camera and laptop.

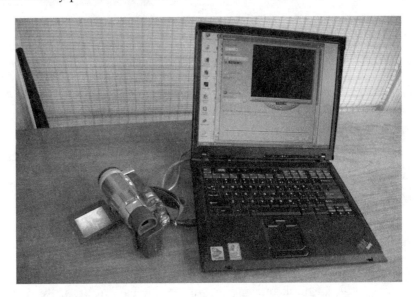

> **tip**   *The fastest way to transfer video from a camera to a laptop is via a FireWire cable. If your laptop doesn't have a FireWire port, and many do not, a USB cable will do the trick—just a bit slower. It's also possible to add a FireWire port to your laptop with a PC Card (see Figure 12-2).*

Figure 12-2

Use a PC Card to add FireWire to your notebook.

Step 3: Hit Record

Now it's time to load the video clips onto your laptop. In the Tasks menu on the left, click on *Capture Video | Capture from video device*. (Alternatively, you can click on *File | Capture Video*). This will launch the Video Capture Wizard.

Step 4: Choose Your Weapon

In the Available Devices page, choose your camera.

Step 5: Add Your Name and Address

Next, choose a name for the video project and a location to save it on your hard drive.

Step 6: Choose Quality vs. Quantity

Before we can actually transfer video from the camera to the laptop, we'll need to decide what type of file to save it as; remember, the higher the quality, the more disk space it will require and the longer it will take the program to process it. Nevertheless, these are our precious memories, so we'll choose *Best Quality* (see Figure 12-3).

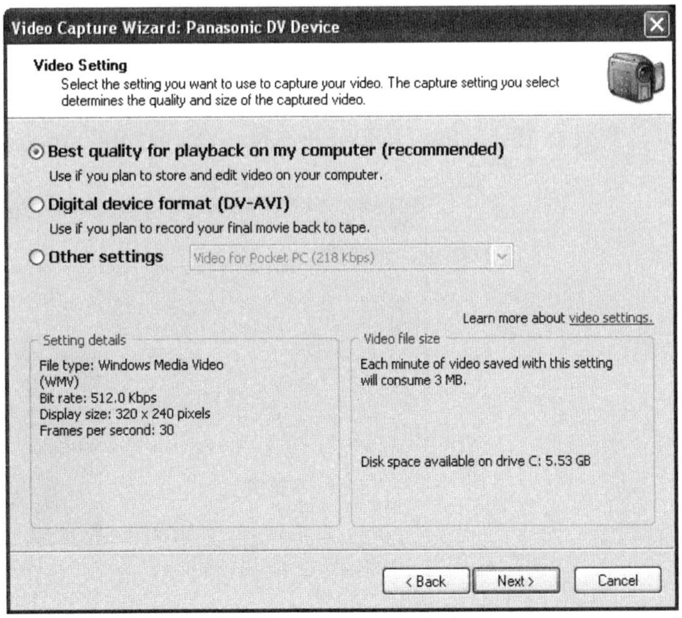

Figure 12-3

Only the best for our footage.

Step 7: Take Only What You Need

Rather than capture the whole tape at once, which would require a lot of time and hard drive space, we're going to capture only the specific clips we want to use in our video. So we'll choose the manual option here (see Figure 12-4).

Figure 12-4

We'll capture only the clips we want to use.

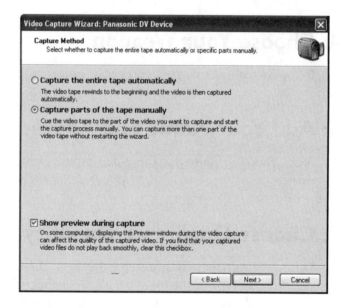

Step 8: Capture the Clips

OK, it's time to start capturing our footage. Using the camera controls underneath the preview window, locate the video segment you want to capture from your camera. Once you've found it, pause it at the beginning, click the *Start Capture* button (see Figure 12-5), and click pause again to get the tape rolling again.

Figure 12-5

Start Capture...

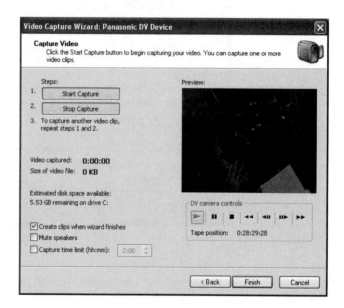

When you come to the end of the clip you want, click the *Stop Capture* button. It's as easy as that. The program will automatically save the captured clip.

Now, capture the next segment, repeating the start and stop process. When you're done capturing all of the segments you want to use, click *Finish* to close the Video Capture Wizard.

Step 9: Put Your Clips in Order

All of your clips should now be arrayed in the collection window. Next, drag each of them, in the order you want them to play, into the timeline at the bottom of the window (see Figure 12-6). The clips will play from left to right.

If you don't care about adding fancy transitions or titles, you can skip straight to Step 12 and burn the DVD.

Excellent! The hard part is over.

Figure 12-6

Put your clips into order.

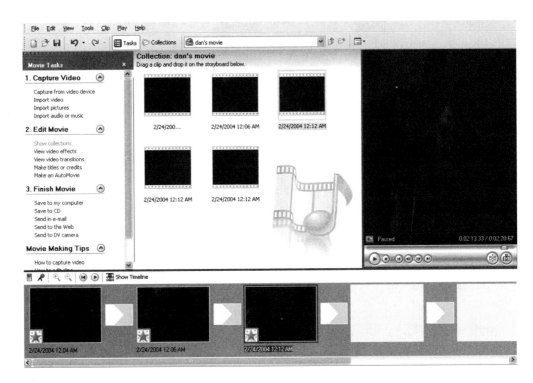

Step 10: Add Special Effects

Now we'll add transitions so that the clips flow smoothly from one to the next. Click on *Tools | View Transitions*. There are over 60 to choose from; some of our favorites include *Dissolve* and *Fade*, but they're all pretty cool (see Figure 12-7).

Figure 12-7

Choose your transition.

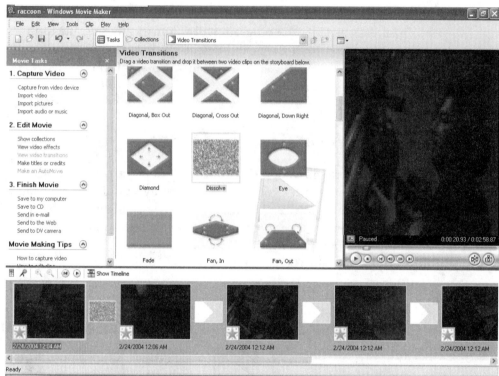

Just drag the transition you want to use onto the small boxes between the clips.

Step 11: Add Titles and Credits

What movie would be worth watching if you didn't know what it was or who was in it? Go to *Tools | Titles and Credits,* and choose when you'd like to have the credits appear on the screen—at the beginning or the end of the movie, or at the front of each clip (see Figure 12-8).

Two text boxes will come up, for the main title and the subtitle. As you type, you'll be able to preview your text on the screen to the right (see Figure 12-9).

When you're happy with your titles, click *Done.*

Step 12: Preview and Save

Next, click the play button and look over your work with a critical eye. If you're happy with what you see, click *File | Save Movie File* on a recordable CD, and click *Next.*

Choose a name for your finished movie. Now, you can choose one of many playback settings, depending on how you plan on distributing your video (see Figure 12-10).

We recommend keeping it simple and using the *Best fit for recordable CD* setting (see Figure 12-11).

Figure 12-8

Pick a time for titles.

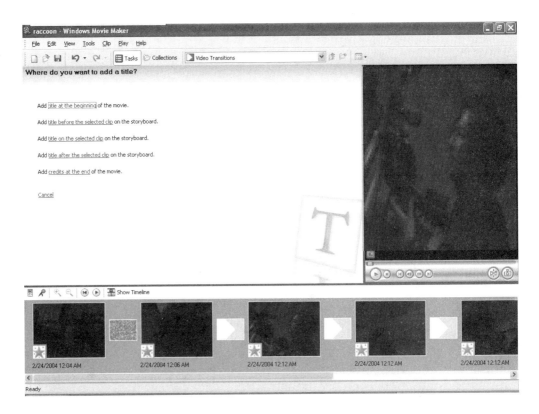

Figure 12-9

Tell them what they're watching.

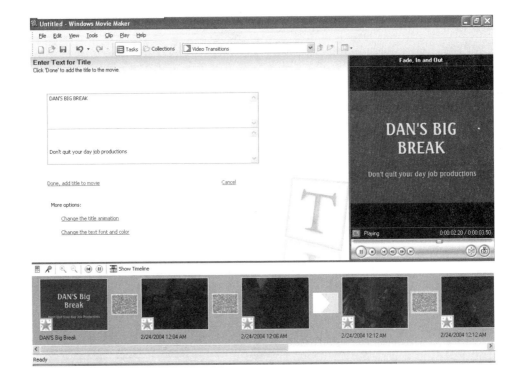

Figure 12-10

Pass the popcorn—
it's preview time.

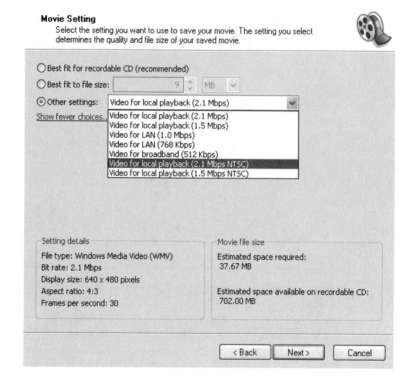

Figure 12-11

Make sure your
movie will fit.

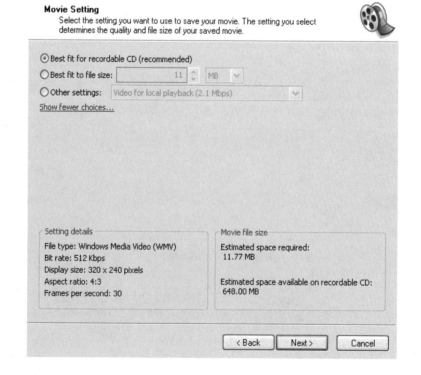

Step 13: Cut! Print!

Click *Next,* and it'll save your film to a disc (see Figure 12-12).

Figure 12-12

Burn, baby, burn.

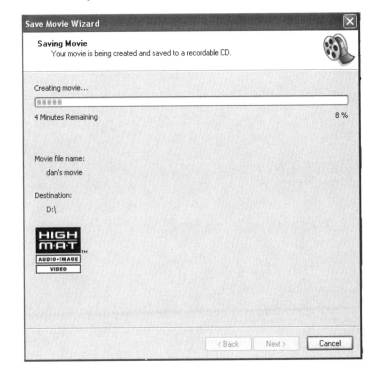

You're done. Next stop—the Oscars.

Project 13

Use Your Fingerprints Instead of Passwords

What You'll Need

- Hardware: Lenovo ThinkPlus Fingerprint Reader
- Software: Included
- Cost: $50 U.S.

Do you feel like you're fighting a losing battle against your ever-expanding list of web site usernames and passwords? Tired of web sites asking for your mother's maiden name or your pet's birthday in order to be e-mailed the account information you forgot? Same here.

The good news is that the solution is just a finger swipe away. That's right, baby; we're going to add a futuristic fingerprint scanner to your laptop. It's called *biometric security*—a method in which you are identified by a unique physical characteristic, in this case, your fingerprint. Most biometric sensors read the electrical characteristics of a fingerprint, making them equally easy to use and hard to fool. (OK, we know what you're thinking: If someone cuts off my finger, will he or she be able to log in to my e-mail? Fortunately, a severed finger will work on most sensors for only a few minutes, after which its electrical properties degrade. Good to know.)

In this chapter, we'll show you how to turn your laptop into a secure, digital vault with Lenovo's ThinkPlus Fingerprint Reader. Instead of having to hunt for your passwords, you'll always have them right at your fingertip.

Step 1: Get Software First

You'll need to install some software before plugging the fingerprint reader into an open USB port on your laptop. Insert the included installation CD and follow the directions (see Figure 13-1). It's also worth checking Lenovo's support web site for newer versions of the software and drivers.

Figure 13-1

Software before hardware.

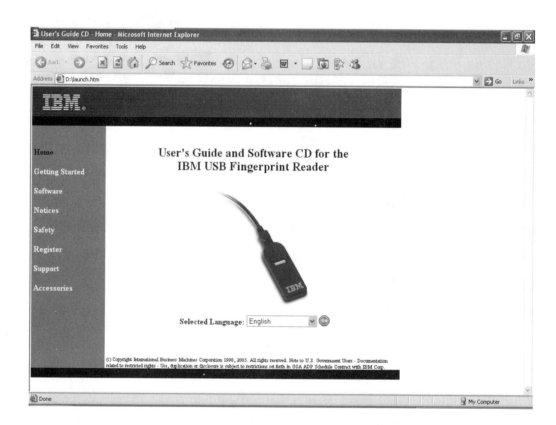

> **note** Besides fingerprint scanners, there are other approaches to laptop security. A popular one among the corporate population is a smart card—a pocket-sized card that has embedded integrated circuits and tamper-resistant properties capable of keeping information confidential. Of course, a smart card can be lost or stolen, while your fingerprints are, well, harder to steal.

Step 2: Secure This

After a quick restart, the software will take over and lead you through the rest of the installation. You'll see that there are many ways to set the device up, depending on how you use your laptop. We're going to assume that, like us, you use it for everything including work, play, and whatever else falls between the two. As such, we're going to set the fingerprint scanner for top security and use it to both to start up the computer and to protect our sensitive files.

All right, we're not taking the easy way out this time: Click on *Advanced configuration* (see Figure 13-2).

Figure 13-2

Forget typical; we're going advanced.

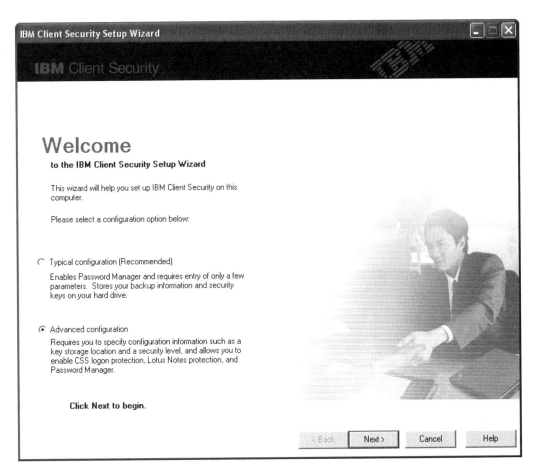

Step 3: Set Your Last Password

You'd think that by installing a fingerprint scanner, we'd be able to quit passwords once and for all from here on out. Well, think again. The first thing the software will ask you to do is create a password—just in case the scanner or software should ever fail, or you need to make changes to either's settings. To maintain top security, the password you choose needs to be at least six characters long, have one number, and not have more than two repeated characters (see Figure 13-3). And, oh yeah, it can't begin or end with a number. (We're still trying to find one that works.) But take comfort in that fact that this is the last password you'll ever have to set.

Step 4: Store Your House Keys

Next, the software asks about where you want to store your administrator keys. Just pick an out-of-the-way location, somewhere on your main hard drive (see Figure 13-4). (Avoid the My Documents folder or the Desktop, as those are the first two places any self-respecting data thief will look.) We recommend that you also archive them in a separate location. A network drive or USB drive makes an excellent depository for the key archive.

Figure 13-3

No more passwords!
OK, one more.

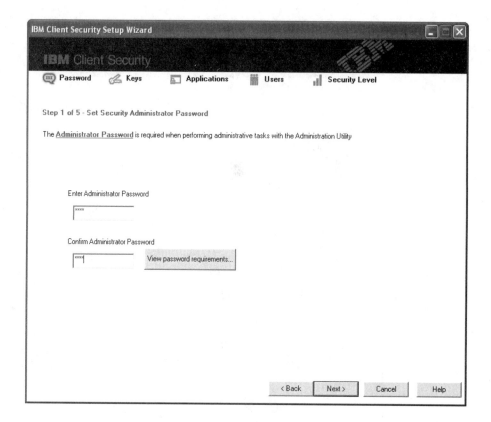

Figure 13-4

Don't forget where you
put your keys.

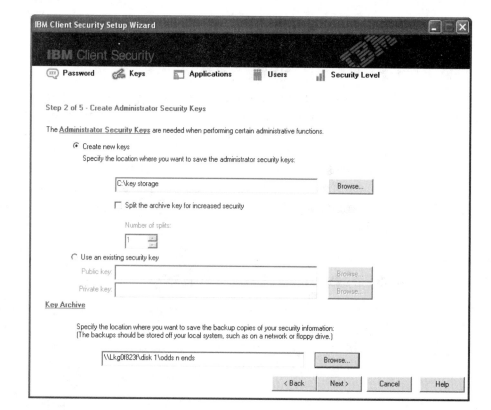

Step 5: Make Some Decisions (And More Decisions)

Egads. This next screen may freak you out if you're not initiated in the arts of security and digital data protection. Let's break it down:

- **Secure access to your system replacing the normal Windows logon with the Client Security secure log on:** Prevents your laptop from starting up unless your fingerprint has been swiped. We like that.

- **Enable file and folder encryption:** Turns all your data into unreadable gibberish until your fingerprint unlocks it. Sounds good to us.

- **Enable IBM Client Security Password Manager support:** Consolidates all of your passwords, which are stored in a secure database. When you scan your finger, the database sends that password out. Oh, yes.

Just think of each check box as another brick in the wall. Make sure the top three are checked; the bottom three should be grayed out (see Figure 13-5).

Figure 13-5

Decide what aspects of protection you want and need.

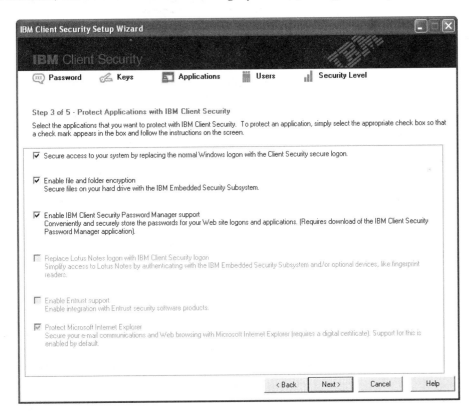

Step 6: Select Security Levels

OK, this step is critical: You need to decide who else will be able to use the laptop besides you. We'll check off *Use UVM passphrase*, which will require each authorized user to create a passphrase. (You'll also need to decide how often you want users to change their passphrases; for now, we'll set it to 90 days.)

Of course, we'll require each authorized user to use the fingerprint reader; they'll all have to register their fingerprint with the scanner.

We'll skip the smart card reader.

Finally, we'll select the level of security we want (see Figure 13-6):

- **Low:** Requires a user to swipe their fingerprint only to start up Windows

- **Medium:** Requires a user to swipe their fingerprint to start up Windows and the first time they open an application

- **High:** Requires a user to swipe their fingerprint to start up Windows and every time they start an application

We recommend selecting the highest setting.

Figure 13-6

Maximum security is your new middle name.

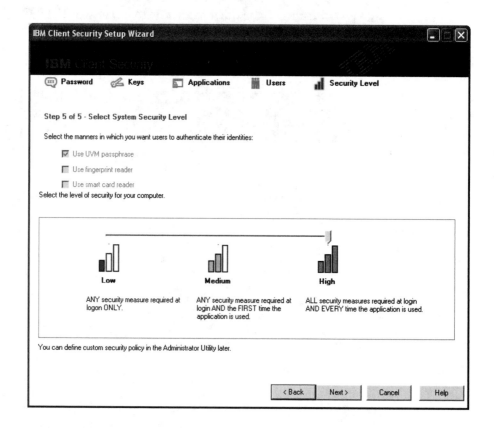

The software will review your choices before turning your computer into an impenetrable fortress (see Figure 13-7).

It'll take some time for the program to digest your settings. Finally, you'll be asked to restart your laptop.

Step 7: Connect the Scanner

Now that the software is all set up, go ahead and connect the fingerprint scanner to an open USB port on your laptop (see Figure 13-8).

Figure 13-7

A last chance to review your settings.

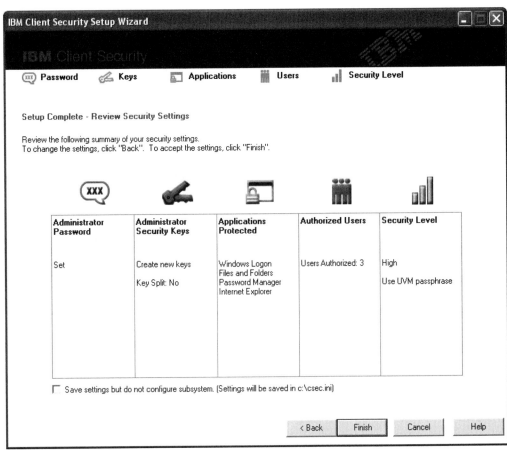

Figure 13-8

Plug in the fingerprint scanner.

Because your security infrastructure now depends on your fingers, pick a few of your favorites (we're partial to pinkies and ring fingers). We suggest registering at least two, one from each hand. And unless you have tiny baby-hands, forget about using your thumbs—those sausages are too big for most scanners.

Step 8: Swipe It

The fingerprint enrollment process may be familiar if you've ever been arrested. Just swipe each finger a few times when prompted to do so (see Figure 13-9).

Figure 13-9

Wait to be invited before you start swiping.

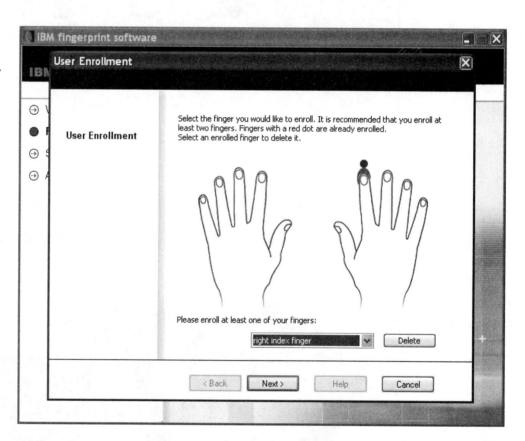

It generally takes four or five tries to get one acceptable scan (see Figure 13-10).

Step 9: Swipe Your Prints

The program will require you to enter three good swipes to register each finger (see Figure 13-11). Be patient.

Figure 13-10

Swipe your fingers to register your prints.

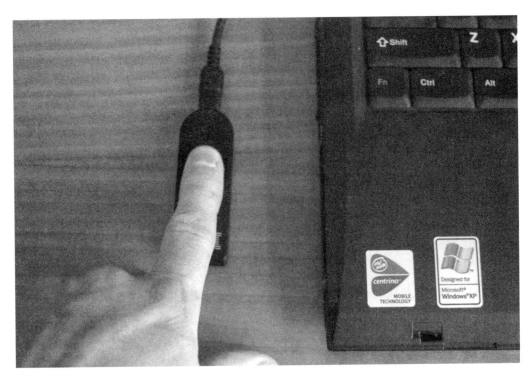

Figure 13-11

Keep swiping until the scanner is happy.

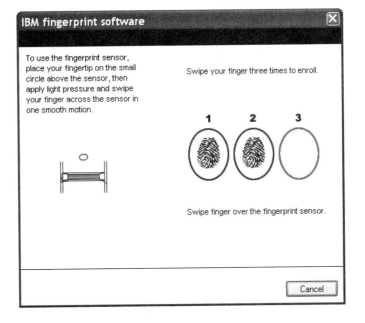

tip   *Some tips for effective swiping: Lightly place the tip of your finger in the circular indentation, keeping it flat and square as you slowly swipe it across the copper-colored band. It'll take some practice. Don't be embarrassed to watch the included demo—it's pretty good (see Figure 13-12).*

Figure 13-12

The interactive tutorial is worthwhile.

Step 10: Scramble Your Files

OK, now that we've registered your fingerprints, it's time to lock down your laptop. The other half of securing your laptop is protecting your files behind an encryption wall. To do this, open a Windows Explorer window and right-click on a file or folder that you want to secure. Then, select *Encrypt this Folder* from the context menu (see Figure 13-13).

Figure 13-13

Send your folder to the crypt.

After you enter your passphrase (the one we created back in Step 6), the computer will get to work scrambling your files. It'll take a few minutes per hundred megabytes.

Then, voilà! No one will be able to open that file without your finger. To decrypt a file, right-click on it, select *Decrypt this file*, and simply swipe your finger.

Step 11: Consolidate Your Passwords

A major advantage of using a fingerprint scanner is that most—if not all—of your passwords can be consolidated. Now, when you access your bank account online, check on your Netflix queue, or log in to your local newspaper's site, all you'll have to do is swipe your finger.

To get set up, click the Password Manager icon in your taskbar—it looks like a padlock (see Figure 13-14).

Figure 13-14

Click on the padlock icon.

Now select *Create*. After authenticating yourself with a swipe of your finger, type in the password you use to access that particular web site, and drag the red-cross hairs to the place on the screen where you normally type in your password. Now save it as a Password Manager Entry (see Figure 13-15).

Figure 13-15

Let the Password Manager remember your passwords from now on.

The next time you try to access the web site, the fingerprint box will automatically pop up. Swipe your finger, and off you go.

Protect Your Laptop from a Data Disaster

What You'll Need

- Hardware: External hard drive
- Software: None
- Cost: $100 U.S. or less

No matter how careful you are with your laptop, accidents happen. Water spills on the keyboard. The motherboard conks out. The hard drive self-destructs. Your mother-in-law drops it. Files are mistakenly deleted. The laptop gets lost or stolen.

While losing your hardware is bad enough, trust us; it's the loss of all of the stuff on it—those photos, years of e-mails, all of your contacts, your entire music collection, the first draft of your novel—that's the true tragedy. Remember, a laptop can be repaired or replaced, but your content is priceless. Not to worry—in this chapter, we're going to show you how to back it all up so that when your laptop meets its maker, as it eventually will, your data will live on to see another day. Fortunately, most laptops come with some sort of backup utility, so all you'll need have a safe place to store your data, such as an external hard drive, a network server, or an online depository. We use an external hard drive—they're relatively inexpensive and easy to deal with, and are an invaluable investment into the security of your digital life.

> **tip** *Many new external hard drives come with backup software already loaded and ready to go. All you have to do is press a single button on the drive, and it'll instantly and automatically create a backup. This is probably the easiest way to back up your system.*

Step 1: Find Some Storage Space

First you need a place to store your stuff. Of course, you could back your data up right on a separate partition of your laptop's hard drive; in case of disaster, you'd have clean, backed-up versions of the files and data that may have gotten corrupted or struck by a virus on your laptop's main drive. But sooner or later the entire hard drive will go bad, or you'll lose your laptop, and you'll be back at square one. An external hard drive, connected via a USB or FireWire port (see Figure 14-1), will keep your data physically separate from your laptop, sort of like a safe deposit box at the bank. Install the drive and its software, and then connect it to your laptop.

Figure 14-1

An external hard drive: a safe deposit box for data.

tip The price of external hard drives continues to plummet. If you have a lot of data, you'll need a big one, but if you're working with a fixed budget, you can save a lot of money by picking up an internal hard drive (made for a desktop or notebook PC) and putting it into an external drive enclosure.

Step 2: Open Your Windows

Next, click on the Windows *Start* button, click on *All Programs, Accessories, System Tools,* and then select *Backup.* The Windows Backup or Restore Wizard will launch (see Figure 14-2).

note Besides the backup program that comes preloaded on most Windows laptops, there are dozens of excellent and simple-to-use backup utilities. You can find many of them reviewed and available for download at www.software.cnet.com and www.download.com.

Step 3: Back Up or Restore?

OK, this one is easy. Before you can restore, you must first back up. Select *Back up files and settings* (see Figure 14-3) and click *Next.* (Later, we'll show you how to restore a dead system.)

Figure 14-2

The Backup or Restore Wizard.

Figure 14-3

You need to back up before you can restore.

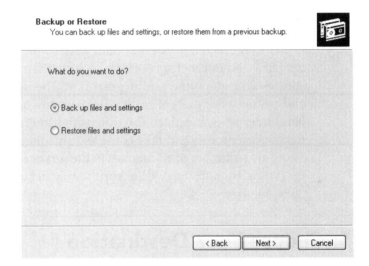

Step 4: Decide How Much Is Enough

Now it's time to choose exactly which files and data you want to back up. You've got four options (see Figure 14-4). You can back up just your documents—that is, only the files that are stored in your My Documents folder—and settings—your bookmarks, saved Internet passwords, and so on; *everything* on the laptop; or just the specific files and folders you choose. Opting to back up only your documents and settings leaves a lot unprotected, and with hard drive space about as cheap as swamp land, we suggest backing up the whole enchilada. In the event that something goes terribly wrong with your laptop, this will make it easy to re-create your entire digital world—not just your data, settings, and bookmarks, but the entire operating system, too.

Figure 14-4

Don't be stingy—back
it all up.

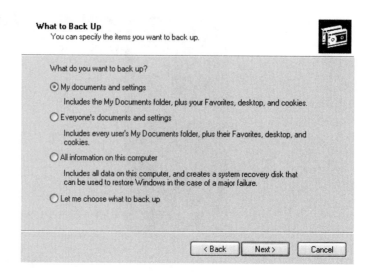

Back Up Online

If you don't have an external hard drive, you can just unload your data on the farm—an Internet server farm. A server farm will keep your data safe and secure—like an online safe deposit box. The upside is that you can back up and restore your system from wherever you are, as long as there's a broadband Internet connection. The downside? Internet server space isn't free, and the backup process can take considerably longer than with an external drive. There are a number of companies in the server farm business, including iBackup (www.ibackup.com), @Backup (www.backup.com), and LiveVault (www.livevault.com).

Step 5: Choose Your Destination

At this point, you need to tell the wizard where to put your backup information. Plug in your external hard drive's letter (see Figure 14-5). You can choose a filename for it, though the program will append the date and time of the backup to whatever name you choose. Click *Next* and then *Finish*.

 Though some backup programs will let you burn your backup files onto CDs or DVDs, they're too small to hold much data and you'll end up baby-sitting the machine and feeding it fresh discs. Most backups require at least 40 GB of space, which is the equivalent of eight DVDs.

Step 6: Make Sure It Fits

The program will go through all of the folders and files that you've asked it to back up and estimate how much hard drive space it'll require (see Figure 14-6). If your hard drive isn't big enough, you'll need to cross some files off the backup list, delete some

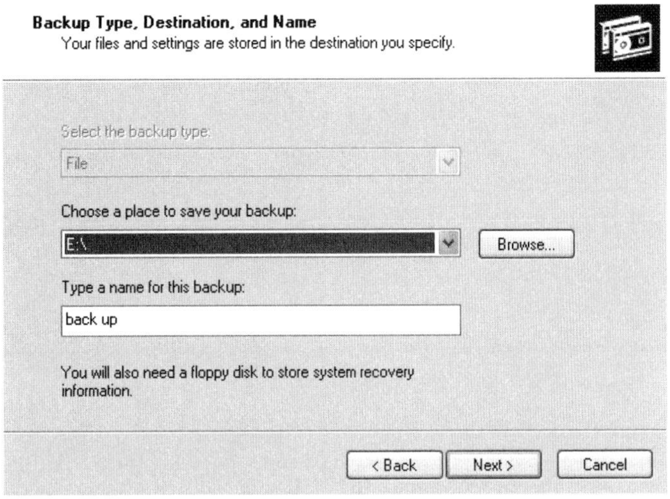

Figure 14-5

Pick a destination and a name for your backup.

Backup Type, Destination, and Name
Your files and settings are stored in the destination you specify.

Select the backup type:

File

Choose a place to save your backup:

E:\   Browse...

Type a name for this backup:

back up

You will also need a floppy disk to store system recovery information.

< Back   Next >   Cancel

stuff from the drive, or get a bigger hard drive. For a laptop with lots of applications and data, the first backup could take a couple of hours; a new machine might take a half hour or so. In other words, after you set it to start, go make a sandwich or something.

Figure 14-6

The program calculates how much room it'll need.

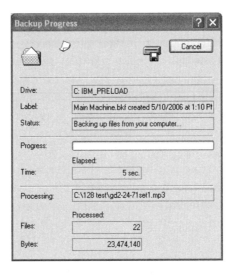

In the Backup Progress dialog box (see Figure 14-7), you'll see a box labeled Estimated remaining time. Ignore it. It's notoriously inaccurate and may fluctuate wildly during the process.

Step 7: Create Your Restore Media

Now it's time to prepare for the worst-case scenario. If your laptop develops a bad system file or catches a virus that keeps it from fully loading up Windows, you're in a scary part of town. The best way to find your way back home is with a *restore disc*. A restore disc contains basic startup information to get Windows jump-started; from

Figure 14-7

Don't count on an accurate estimate.

there, you should be able to repair or reinstall the operating system and then eventually reload all of your backup data from the external hard drive. Some, but not all, laptops come with a restore disc.

If you don't have one, don't despair. We'll make one. Some other backup programs can create a restore disc on a CD or DVD, but Microsoft's backup software requires you to use an old-school floppy disk (yes, a *floppy disk*)! If your laptop has a floppy drive, you're all set; if it doesn't—and most recent-models do not—you'll need to buy one that connects via USB. Fortunately, they're as cheap as dirt.

To make the restore disc, start the Backup or Restore Wizard again, click the *Advanced Mode* link, and choose *Automated System Recovery Wizard*. When the wizard starts up, click *Next*, choose a name for your backup, select a destination for the backup (your external hard drive, or whatever), and click *Finish*. When the utility finishes creating your backup, it will ask if you want to create the disk (see Figure 14-8). Make sure your floppy drive is installed and set up, and has a fresh floppy disk in it. The restore disc shouldn't take more than a minute or two to make. Once it's done, label the disk and put it a safe place. You never know when you'll need to recover from a digital disaster.

Figure 14-8

Create a floppy disk with startup data.

Step 8: Continue to Back Up

Congratulations! You've backed up your laptop and created a recovery disc. Of course, the next time you do *anything*—send or receive an e-mail, bookmark a web site, create or edit a file—your backup is immediately out of date.

Welcome to your new life. From now on, you'll need to periodically update your backup file. Fortunately, this takes a lot less time and effort than that initial backup did, because you're updating only those files and settings that have changed.

Step 9: Go Back to See the Wizard

Open up the Backup Wizard again. Instead of clicking Next, however, select the *Advanced Mode* link. Now click on the *Schedule Jobs* tab. Click on *Add Job*, located in the lower-right corner, and go through Steps 4 and 5 again. Finally, you'll be confronted with a number of options about what type of backup to make:

- **Normal:** Backs up all your files from scratch and marks files as completed.

- **Copy:** Backs up all of your files, but doesn't mark them as backed up.

- **Incremental:** Backs up only the files that were changed since the last backup, and marks files as completed.

- **Differential:** Backs up only the files that were changed since the last backup, but doesn't mark them as backed up.

- **Daily:** Backs up only the files that were changed today.

We recommend choosing the Incremental option; it should be enough to keep you protected. (Don't worry about whether files are marked as complete or not—it's just Windows' internal bookkeeping system to account for what's new and what's old). Make your choice (see Figure 14-9) and click *Next*.

Figure 14-9

Incremental backups should keep you safe.

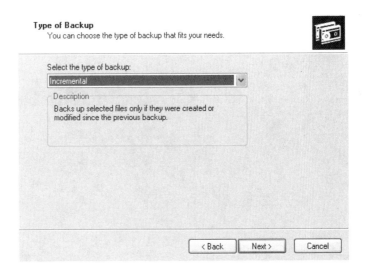

Step 9: Give Your Backup a Checkup

We recommend that you check the box labeled *Verify data after backup*. It's not going to cost you any time, and it's better to be safe than sorry. Go ahead and click *Next* (see Figure 14-10).

Figure 14-10

Verify—just in case.

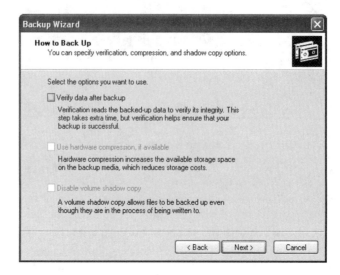

Step 10: Append or Replace

Whenever you back up, you have a choice to build a whole new data set or just add new files to the existing lump. We suggest you append—there's no need to start from scratch every time. That said, it's not a bad idea to start anew every few months, just to keep out any errors that may have crept into your incremental backup.

Step 11: Back Up While You Sleep

Backing up is a thing best done late at night, when you're not using your laptop. Click *Later*, and then select the *Set Schedule* button. Set the *Schedule Task* to *Daily*, and pick a start time—preferably a late time, like 1 A.M. (see Figure 14-11). (Make sure it doesn't conflict with your antivirus scan time.) Click *Finish*. Now you can wake up refreshed and guilt-free.

Figure 14-11

Enter the time when you want the backup to start.

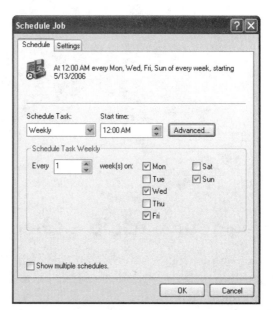

After the first few backups, it's a good idea to look at the file and make sure it's working. Where you put your data backups is as important as having them in the first place. Consider keeping your external hard drive and laptop separated when you're not backing up, so that a disaster is less likely to hit them both simultaneously.

Restoring Your Laptop

Whatever tragedy has struck your laptop is unimportant. Your data is safe and secure because you backed your system up 24 hours ago on an external hard drive. You may be missing a few recent e-mails and files, but you're going to get everything else back. Thank yourself for being smart enough to back up your data.

 If your laptop is acting unstable or some applications aren't working properly, before restoring the system with your backed-up files, try a System Restore. Click on the Windows Start button, then All Programs, Accessories, System Tools, and then System Restore. Select Restore my computer to an earlier time. Then, pick a date and restore point (see Figure 14-12). System Restore lets you roll back Windows system files, registry keys, and installed programs to a previous state in the event of a failure. In Windows Vista, System Restore has been renamed to System Protection.

Figure 14-12

Sometimes System Restore is all it takes to get your laptop back on its feet.

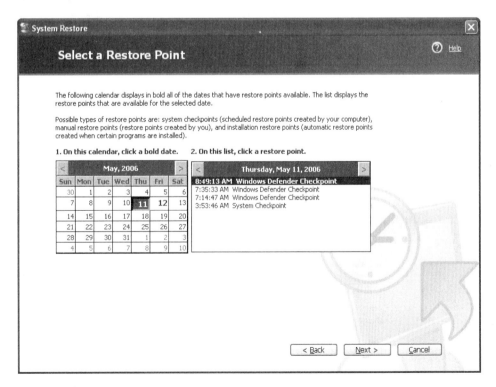

If you've got a new laptop, or your old laptop is in good enough shape to boot Windows, you're halfway home. Launch the Backup and Restore Wizard (outlined in Step 2) and select *Restore files and settings* (see Figure 14-13).

Select the backup file you want to restore; if you're faced with a number of choices, try the most recent one first. If your laptop can't boot Windows, you'll need to use the restore discs you created. To do this, you may have to go into the BIOS settings, to tell your laptop to access the floppy drive first when it starts up; otherwise, it'll go to the hard drive with the bad data and you won't go anywhere. To change your BIOS settings, start your computer and keep your eyes peeled; before Windows starts, your laptop will display some startup information and offer you a chance to change the BIOS settings; generally, you press the F2 or F4 key—quickly, now—before Windows starts. Once inside the inner sanctum of your computer, you'll see something like *Boot Order* or *Drives*. You'll need to configure it so that the floppy disk drive is at the top of the list.

Figure 14-13

Bring your laptop back from the dead.

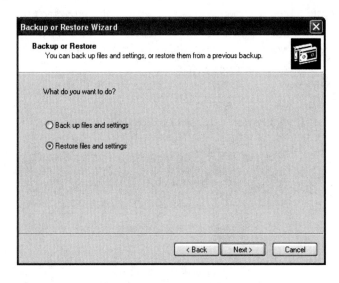

Make Your Laptop Safe for Surfing

What You'll Need:

- **Hardware: A broadband Internet connection**
- **Windows Software: AntiVirus (PC Tools Software), Defender (Microsoft), CYBERsitter (Solid Oak Software), KidRocket (KidRocket.org)**
- **Mac Software: AntiVirus for Mac (Norton), Virex, and Intego Virus Barrier X4 (Norton)**
- **Cost: Free (or free to try) to $100 U.S.**

The World Wide Web is a wonderland for those curious and patient enough to explore the enchanting, educational, and entertaining nuggets nestled within its billions of sites. It's also a dangerous place for kids (and adults) who are too trusting or ignorant to recognize the hazards. Behind the veil of many innocuous-looking web sites lies a shadow world overflowing with viruses, spyware, adware, predators, and pornography. Unfortunately, most computers come ill-equipped to deal with the onslaught, and there's no single piece of software that can protect against all of the threats. In this chapter, we'll help you find and set up four programs that will protect your laptop and make the Web a safe and fun place for both kids and adults.

note *The term* World Wide Web *is often mistakenly used as a synonym for the Internet itself, but the Web is actually a service that operates over the Internet, just like e-mail. Technically, the Web is the complete set of documents and media residing on all Internet servers that use the HTTP protocol.*

First, we'll install a virus and spyware scanner to offer protection against the sneaky, malicious programs and web sites that can screw up your laptop royally. Second, we'll set up filtering software to help steer you and your kids away from dangerous sites.

Third, we'll load up a filtering and monitoring application that will both steer you and your children away from objectionable content and let you know exactly where your kids (and anyone else who uses your laptop) are spending their time online. Finally, to prevent the family laptop from becoming a prison with a screen, we'll install a kid-friendly browser.

The good news is that each of the programs we'll show you are free—at least to try; download them from the vendor's site, install them, and you're protected. The bad news is that the essential updates that keep up these programs up to date generally only last for a month or less—and when your time runs out, you'll have to shell out cold hard cash to keep them. Still, we recommend that you give each of them a try; spend a few days with them, and decide which of them work for you before you pay any fees.

We believe that these programs make it easier for a family to enjoy all the good things that the Web has to offer.

Step 1: Vaccinate Your Laptop

You may want to sit down for this. Your laptop came from the factory exposed to all kinds of viral assaults from countless hackers who are just waiting to invade, cripple, and take it over. It may have come with a trial version of an antivirus program, which needs to be installed, configured, and kept up-to-date. If yours didn't come with an antivirus application, or you didn't bother setting up the one that did, don't fret. There are dozens of programs that offer competent protection, but our favorite is PC Tools AntiVirus for Windows, which you can download at www.download.com or www.pctools.com/anti-virus. Go ahead and download the file, and then double-click it to install the program.

note We're partial to PC Tools AntiVirus, but there are many other competent applications on the market; for up-to-date reviews and recommendations of antivirus software, check out www .download.com or www.software.cnet.com.

Step 2: Update the Virus Database

The viruses infecting the Web are constantly changing, with new variants appearing nightly; to remain vigilant and effective, your antivirus software must receive frequent updates so it can be on the lookout for the newest and nastiest specimens; PC Tools' trial subscription includes a month of free updates. Once you've installed the application, it's critical that you update its virus database so that it can scan for (and guard against) new viruses. Just click on the *Smart Update* button to open the Smart Update dialog box (see Figure 15-1). The rest is automatic. If you're compulsive, feel free to run the update daily; otherwise, a weekly update should do the trick.

Figure 15-1

Update the software's virus database.

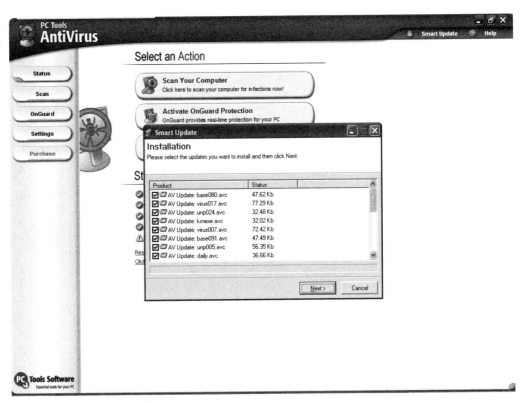

Step 3: Give Your Hard Drive a Checkup

Believe it or not, some new computers come fresh from the factory infected with viruses. And even if your laptop was born clean, it won't stay that way for long. In fact, if you've been practicing "unprotected surfing," you're likely to have picked up an infection or two somewhere along the way. Don't worry—we won't judge you.

To start, it's essential that you let AntiVirus scan every file that's on your laptop. The program will compare every file that's on your hard drive against its database of known viruses. Databases range from a few thousand entries to hundreds of thousands; PC Tools AntiVirus has approximately 200,000 virus signatures on file, and adds more every day. Depending on the size of your hard drive and how many files you have stored on it, the scan can take anywhere from a few minutes to an hour (see Figure 15-2).

tip *Network drives, external hard drives, flash cards, and any other storage devices that are connected to your laptop will extend your scan time. At first, we recommend doing a scan of all of the gadgets that you regularly connect to your laptop. If you want to speed up subsequent scans, however, you can use the Custom Scan option to focus on just your laptop's hard drive.*

Figure 15-2

Start by scanning
the hard drive for
live viruses.

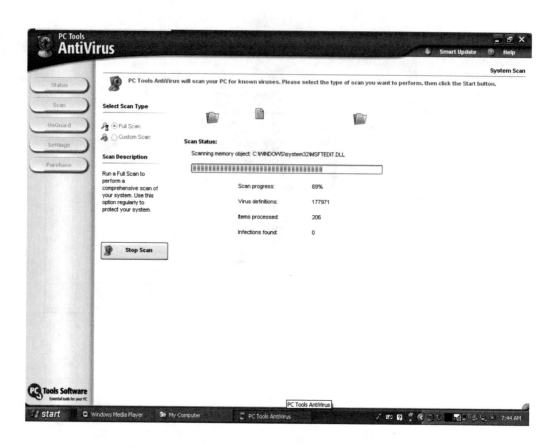

Step 4: Activate Security

Virus software can be a double-edged sword: Set to its most aggressive level, it will catch even the sneakiest intruder—but it may also keep your computer so busy that it will slow down to a grinding halt. AntiVirus's OnGuard treads relatively lightly on your processor, but still manages to examine every new file that touches your machine (see Figure 15-3), from that e-mail message about the luscious Russian woman looking for a husband to the web site that promises to triple your money overnight.

Still, if OnGuard is gumming up the works, you can quickly disable it for a period of time—or completely (see Figure 15-4).

Step 5: Scan While You Sleep

The process of scanning for viruses can really slow a computer down, so it's best to avoid scanning when you're sitting in front of your laptop, playing online poker against someone in Taiwan. Fortunately, most modern antivirus programs let you schedule scans for any time of day or night (see Figure 15-5). We recommend that you set your antivirus software to download the latest virus signatures and scan the hard drive when you're not using it—like 3 A.M. College students may prefer to set it for the later morning hours.

Figure 15-3

OnGuard protects by screening all new files.

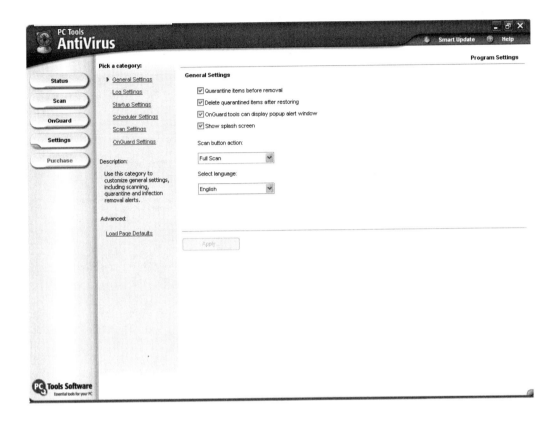

Figure 15-4

OnGuard can be easily turned off.

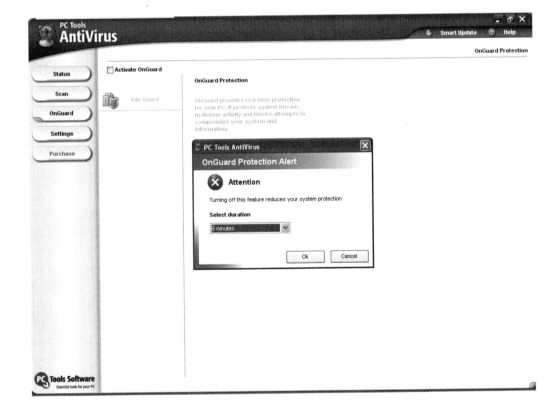

Figure 15-5

Schedule your scanning for sleepytime.

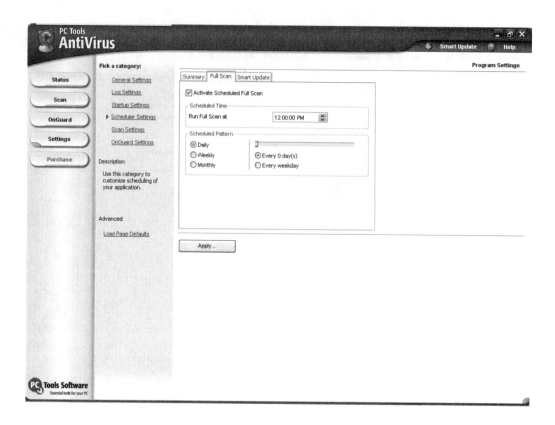

Step 6: Declare War on Malware

As if viruses weren't bad enough, the Web is run amok with other pitfalls such as *spyware* and *adware*. These nasty programs, which may subtly install themselves while you're innocently visiting a web site or downloading a file, can reassign your web browser's home page, add unseemly sites to your bookmarks or favorites list, slow your laptop down to a crawl, or worse. In fact, if your laptop is running sluggishly,

Macintoshes and Viruses

With 95 percent of all computers in circulation running some version of Microsoft's operating system, Windows PCs are the favorite target of virus writers and malware producers. That said, if your laptop is running Apple's Macintosh operating system, you're not totally out of harm's way. Whether it's a virus or Java script that's programmed to wipe out your hard drive, the danger is just as real for Mac users, too. The top-selling antivirus programs for Macs include Norton AntiVirus (www.symantec.com), McAfee Virex (www.mcafee.com), and Intego VirusBarrier (www.intego.com). They're all fairly similar to PC-based virus applications, scanning the hard drive for destructive software and deleting malignant files. Unfortunately, they're often more expensive and don't always offer a free trial period.

your web browser keeps going back to a certain site, or you see other unexplained phenomena, chances are you've been hit by one or more of these programs. The solution: Get and install an antispyware program.

note   Spyware *is malicious software designed to intercept or take partial control of a computer without the informed consent of that computer's owner or legitimate user.* Adware *is software that automatically plays, displays, or downloads advertising material to a computer after the software is installed on it or while the application is being used. Both spyware and adware are kinds of* malware, *defined as any type of software that's designed to infiltrate or damage a computer system.*

There are many antispyware applications to choose from, but we like Microsoft Windows Defender, which you can download at www.microsoft/athome/security/ spyware/software. Go ahead and download the file, and then double-click the Defender icon to install the program. Take note that before you can use Defender, you'll need to make sure your copy of Windows is up to date—a good thing to do periodically, anyway—and licensed. To update Windows, visit www.update.microsoft.com and follow the directions.

note   *We like Microsoft Windows Defender, but there are plenty of other counterinsurgency programs out there. Anyway, for up-to-date reviews and recommendations of antispyware software, check out www.download.com or www.software.cnet.com.*

Like the antivirus tool, Defender needs to be updated with the latest definitions to protect your laptop effectively (see Figure 15-6).

Figure 15-6

Update Defender's spyware definitions.

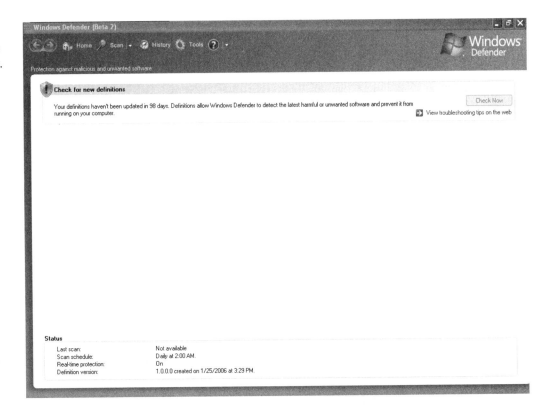

Once it has scanned your laptop for malware and uninstalled, quarantined, or destroyed whatever it's found, go ahead and celebrate. When you're done with that, click the *Tools* tab, select *Options*, and set the automatic scanning and default actions to fit your online lifestyle. In addition, we suggest that you check the box to enable real-time protection (see Figure 15-7), which will alert you if you're in danger of exposing your laptop to bad software. There are options to protect many of the different parts of your laptop; we recommend that you activate them all, and turn any off that cramp your style.

Figure 15-7

Real-time protection will watch your back.

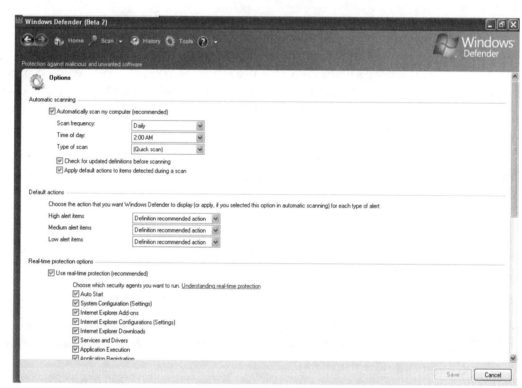

note   *Defender's Software Explorer, also located in the Options section, lets you see what programs are automatically launched when you turn on your laptop. If your laptop runs slower than it used to, weed out any unnecessary impediments.*

Step 7: Find a Good Cybernanny

Even if you're conscientious about keeping your antivirus and antispyware programs up-to-date, it's still an uphill battle to keep kids protected from the Web's seamier side. You can't always be looking over their shoulders, but you can set some limits with a filtering and monitoring program. Thanks to a built-in database of safe sites and an ability to assess new sites for objectionable material, Solid Oak Software's CYBERsitter program can keep kids surfing on the straight and narrow. You can download the software for free at www.download.com or www.cybersitter.com, but the trial lasts only 10 days. Go ahead and download the file, and then double-click it to install the program.

 We think your kids are in good hands with CYBERsitter, but there are many other monitoring and filtering programs available online; for up-to-date reviews and recommendations of them, check out www.download.com or www.software.cnet.com.

Step 8: Clean House: Setting Limits

After you install it, CYBERsitter will search your hard drive for "suspicious" material, and give you the option to keep or delete whatever it finds (see Figure 15-8).

Figure 15-8

CYBERsitter searches your hard drive for dubious material.

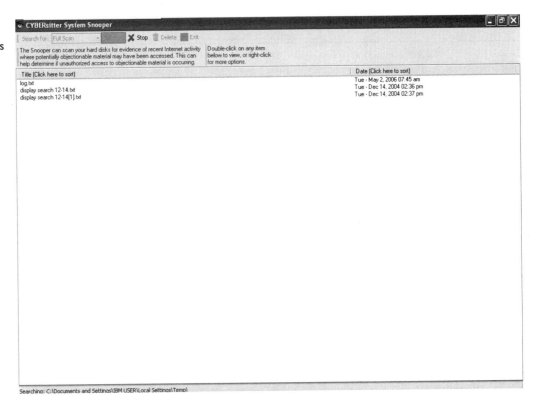

CYBERsitter doesn't get to decide what's objectionable—that's your job. You can configure the program's list of potentially objectionable categories and custom-design your own defense. Out of the nearly two dozen categories, just check off what you want to keep your kids away from. We think that sites on the "Hate and Intolerance" list are probably worth avoiding for web surfers of any age, but "Social Networking Sites" and "Tattoo and Piercing" are judgment calls for you to make (see Figure 15-9). The company offers periodic updates to the list, so check back with them every so often.

Figure 15-9

You decide what's off-limits.

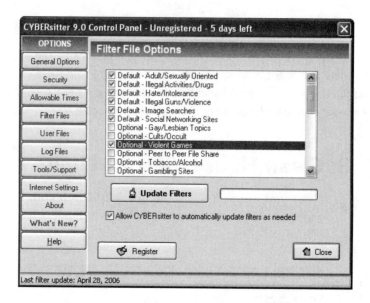

CYBERsitter also offers a convenient way to set time limits for web surfing (see Figure 15-10).

Figure 15-10

There's no arguing with CYBERsitter's allowable access time function.

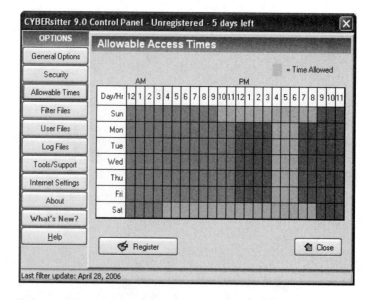

Step 9: Keep It Simple, Keep It Safe

Teens may thrive on the unconstrained power of mainstream browsers such as Microsoft Internet Explorer, Netscape Navigator, and Mozilla Firefox, but these programs can be a bit too much for little kids who are just looking to spend some quality time with Barney. To make the Web a simpler place to play and learn, we like the KidRocket browser (see Figure 15-11), available at www.kidrocket.org. This one's free, although the developers ask for a donation if you like the program.

Figure 15-11

A simpler Web.

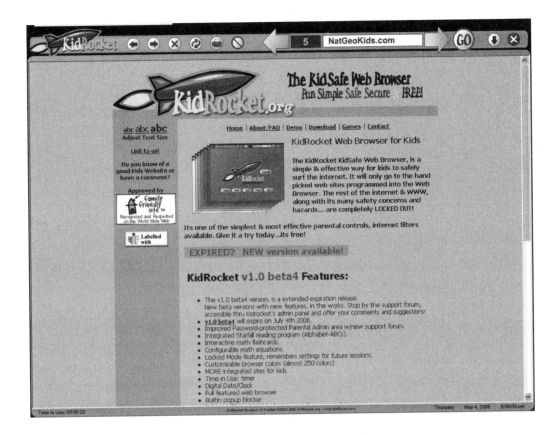

KidRocket comes preloaded with 13 kid-safe sites. All your child has to do is click the arrows located on either side of the address bar and click *Go* (see Figure 15-12).

Figure 15-12

Go means, you know, go.

Sometimes less is more. KidRocket has fewer controls than mainstream browsers, big, simple buttons, and fewer navigational choices. The buttons get even bigger when you scroll over them (see Figure 15-13).

Figure 15-13

Bigger buttons are fun.

 We think KidRocket is ideal for young children, but there are a number of other kid-tuned browsers around; for up-to-date reviews and recommendations, check out www.download.com or www.software.cnet.com.

Project 16
Navigate a Road Trip

What You'll Need

- Hardware: DeLorme Earthmate LT-20 GPS receiver, Velcro
- Software: Street Atlas USA (included)
- Cost: $75 to $100 U.S.

Whether you've got an uncanny sense of direction or—like us—you have trouble finding the bathroom in your own house, it never hurts to have a buddy who's good with maps. In this chapter, we'll introduce you (and your laptop) to some especially good navigational friends to have—namely, the global positioning satellites that make up the global positioning system, more often known by its initials—GPS.

Born of the cold war conflict with the Soviet Union, GPS was developed by the United States Department of Defense to target missiles and track soldier movement. In the 1980s, it was opened up for civilian use, and now GPS devices are commonly found in rental cars, delivery trucks, and even the pockets of hikers, helping people figure out where they're going.

In this chapter, we'll be using an inexpensive GPS receiver, the DeLorme Earthmate LT-20, to give our laptop mapping and routing abilities. So go ahead and chuck your compass, sextant, and paper maps into the basement. You're about to join the GPS club.

Step 1: Choose the Setup: S, M, or L

To get started, we'll install the mapping software from the two CDs that comes with the package. If you're running low on disk space, load the compact setup. Otherwise, go for the typical setup that includes the full set of Points of Interest, which include restaurants, gas stations, parks, cash machines, and more (see Figure 16-1). Or, choose the Custom install, and take only what you want. The whole process should take no more than 15 minutes.

Figure 16-1

Just the maps, all the facts, or in between—you decide.

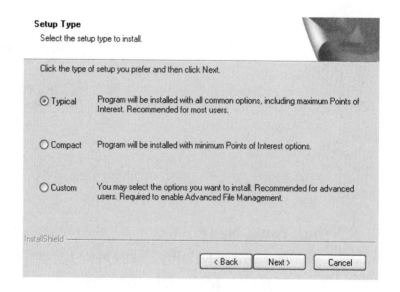

Setup Type
Select the setup type to install.

Click the type of setup you prefer and then click Next.

⊙ Typical   Program will be installed with all common options, including maximum Points of Interest. Recommended for most users.

○ Compact   Program will be installed with minimum Points of Interest options.

○ Custom   You may select the options you want to install. Recommended for advanced users. Required to enable Advanced File Management.

InstallShield

[< Back] [Next >] [Cancel]

note *GPS receivers come in all shapes and sizes. In addition to connecting via USB, you can find GPS receivers that slip into a PC Card or CompactFlash slot or connect wirelessly via Bluetooth. There are more expensive devices that are made expressly for car dashboards and self-contained, hand-held units that can fit into a pocket; even some cell phones are outfitted with GPS capabilities.*

Step 2: Load the Mapping Data

Near the end of the installation routine, a window will pop up: Do you want to put all of the maps directly onto your hard drive (see Figure 16-2)? The mapping data, which includes every side street, avenue, and highway from Maine to California, will take up a little more than half a gigabyte of space. Unless you're really strapped for megabytes, we say go for it—the program will run faster and you won't have to dig up the CD to map out regions you didn't originally install.

Figure 16-2

If you can spare the space, load it all.

Street Atlas USA 2006 - InstallShield Wizard   ⊠

ⓘ   Installing the program road data to your hard drive lets you use Street Atlas USA 2006 without the data disc (645 MB hard disk space required). To launch the data setup, click OK to close this message and then insert the Program Data disc into your CD-ROM drive once the blue screen disappears.

[OK]

Step 3: Get Hooked Up

Now connect the GPS receiver to an open USB port on your laptop (see Figure 16-3). The hardware and software should find each other. (If you run into any problems, DeLorme's web site has a slew of troubleshooting tips.)

Figure 16-3

Plug in your
GPS receiver.

Step 4: Find Yourself

OK, we're all set to go outside for a test run. You can give it a go in your house, but GPS works best out in the open—especially in places where there aren't too many walls, trees, or tall buildings that might obstruct your communication with the satellites. Start the DeLorme software; once the program gets oriented, you should see a map, and exactly where you are on it—in our case, at the moment, near Pelham, NY (see Figure 16-4).

tip *At the bottom of the screen, in your instrument panel, the receiver's LED will blink red while it tries to connect with the satellites (see Figure 16-5); a yellow light means it has acquired your location; and green shows that it has your location and your altitude. Be patient: It can take a few minutes for it to warm up and get oriented. If that red light keeps blinking, here are a few things to try:*

- Click on the *GPS* box along the bottom of the map, click on *Exchange*, and make sure the *Com Port* is set to USB (see Figure 16-6).

- Move to a location with more open sky.

- Disconnect the receiver and plug it back in.

- Restart your laptop.

Figure 16-4

The green dot represents your location on the map.

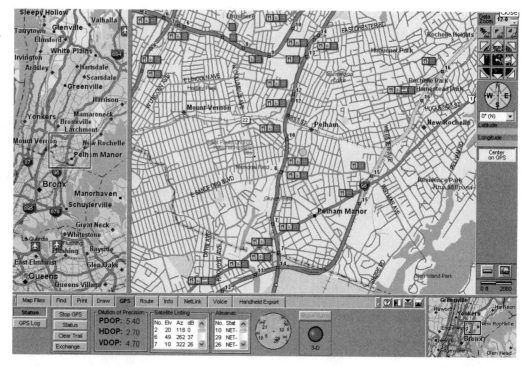

Figure 16-5

Your GPS status light.

Figure 16-6

Set the Com Port to USB.

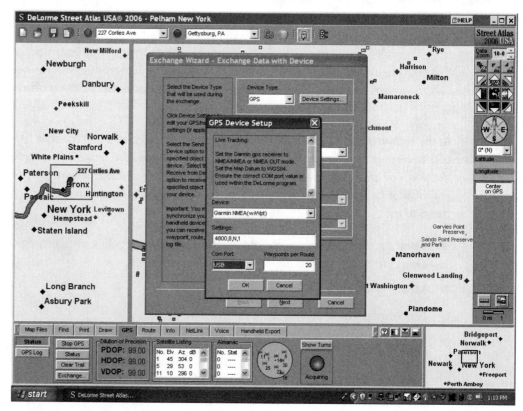

Step 5: Get Oriented

Once the GPS hardware has located you, let's get you oriented within the Street Atlas USA software.

At the top of the main interface window, you'll see a green circle and a red circle, each with a white text field next to it (see Figure 16-7). These text fields are where you type in your starting point and destination.

In the upper-right corner, you'll see a globe split into pieces with yellow arrows (see Figure 16-8); this is for zooming in and out, and reorienting the map.

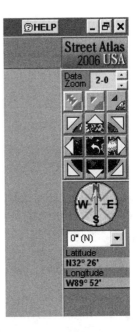

Just below are a compass and the exact longitude and latitude readings for your current position; kind of neat, but not of much use to the casual traveler. More interesting is the red status strip that runs along the lower-left corner of the map window, which shows the location of the cursor—road name, state, and ZIP code. Also notice the thumbnail image in the lower-right corner, which shows a larger portion of whichever map you're looking at, with the detailed area outlined in red.

Street Atlas USA has a bunch of shortcuts for navigating around the map. For example, instead of clicking on yellow arrows to zoom in, you can press ALT+PAGE DOWN *(*ALT+PAGE UP *zooms back out). You can also move the cursor to the edge of the current map, in the direction you want to go, until a white hand shows up; the program will reorient the map in that direction.*

Step 6: Find a Location

OK, now that the satellites know where we are, and we know our way around the software, it's time to take this operation to the streets. Before you pull out of your driveway, however, take a moment to find good spots in your car for the GPS receiver and laptop. The receiver can go either on top of the dashboard, where its rubberized base will keep it anchored during sharp turns, or onto the base of the windshield via its suction cup. Wherever you put it, it must have an unhindered view of the sky.

A smaller laptop will sometimes fit nicely on a lowered glove-compartment door (see Figure 16-9). This setup also accommodates room for an assistant navigator to sit shotgun so that the driver can concentrate on, well, driving.

Figure 16-9

Put your laptop on the glove-compartment door...

If your laptop's too big for that, or the glove compartment is too small, you can place the laptop notebook on top of the console between the two front seats (see Figure 16-10); a little bit of Velcro may help to secure it even better.

As a last resort, if your laptop screen opens wide enough, slide the keyboard down between the two front seats and leave the display sticking up (see Figure 16-11).

If all else fails, throw your laptop in the back seat.

Figure 16-10

...or on the shelf between the front seats...

Figure 16-11

...or jam it between the front seats.

caution Wherever you put the laptop, do not *look at the screen* or type in commands while driving. When in doubt as to where you are or where you are going, pull over to the side of the road and figure it out. Studies have shown that drivers looking at a GPS screen or talking on a cell phone are more accident-prone than drivers who are drunk. The few seconds you may gain by multitasking could cost you your life or someone else's.

Step 7: Let's Get Going

Yes! Finally, everything's all set up. Let's hit the road. We'll be going from Westchester County, New York to Gettysburg, Pennsylvania to soak up some Civil War history.

> **tip** The Street Atlas USA software has a provision for adding stops to your car trip. Just click the Route box near the bottom of the screen and, in the box marked Stop, type in the location of the stop you want to make. Or, if you're already on the road, right-click on the map where you want to stop, and click Stop on the context menu. The route will change instantly to accommodate your wanderlust. Best of all, if you make a wrong turn, the software will automatically recalculate the directions to your destination.

Step 8: Speak to Me

When you're trying to figure out where you're going, the only thing better than looking at a map is having someone dictate the directions to you. Fortunately, our GPS unit can do just this. After you enter your start and end destinations and the software charts your course (see Figure 16-12), click the *Voice* tab at the bottom of the window and select *Voice tab commands*. Now, the software will tell you—out loud—exactly when it's time to make a turn; you can even ask it for specific directions such as "show next turn" or "zoom in."

Figure 16-12

The route is set.

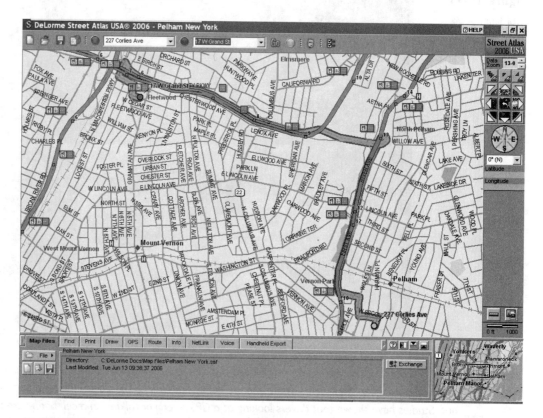

That's it—you're off on your road trip, with your trusty GPS literally telling you where to go. Drive safely.

Part III

Advanced

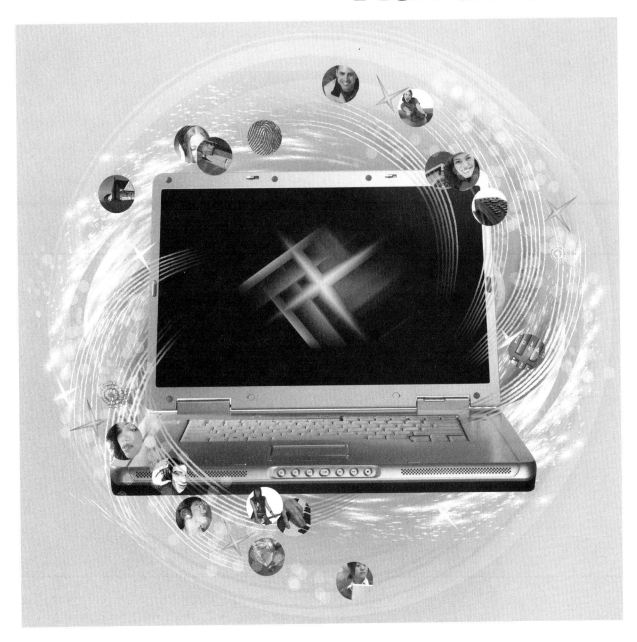

Build a Home
Security System

What You'll Need

- Hardware: Linksys WVC54GC Wireless-G video camera, wireless network and router, Ethernet cable
- Software: SoloLink DDNS; Internet browser
- Cost: $75 U.S.

There's nothing more important than the safety of your family and your home. While you can't always be there to protect them, with your laptop and a webcam, you can always keep an eye on them. In this chapter we'll build a flexible home security system that you can use in a number of ways:

- Watch your front door when you're at work (or on vacation)
- Watch your kids (or roommates) while you're away
- Watch the nanny who's watching your kids while you're away
- Watch your car when it's parked on the street
- Watch the sidewalk in front of your house, just to see who walks by
- Monitor your kids' (or roommates') TV or Internet activity

The great thing is that you don't have to be in front of your own laptop to watch the security video feed; you can monitor it from any PC with Internet access—at work, from an Internet café, anywhere.

Though you can use any kind of webcam to build a home security system, we'll use the Linksys WVC54GC Wireless-G video camera and included software package; though this camera has a lower resolution than others, it's wireless, which makes it easier to move around the house and a little less conspicuous.

Step 1: Set Up the Software First

First we'll set up the camera's software. Put the CD that came with the camera into your laptop's drive. Once the installation wizard launches, click *Next* (see Figure 17-1). It shouldn't take too long for the installation to complete.

Figure 17-1

Start up the software.

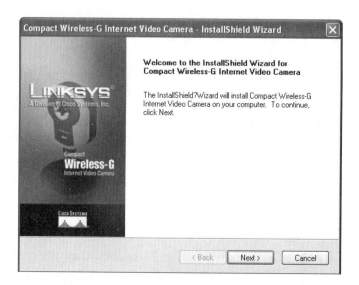

Step 2: Connect That Camera

Now, when prompted, connect the camera to your wireless network router using the Ethernet cable (see Figure 17-2).

Figure 17-2

Connect the camera to the router with an Ethernet cable.

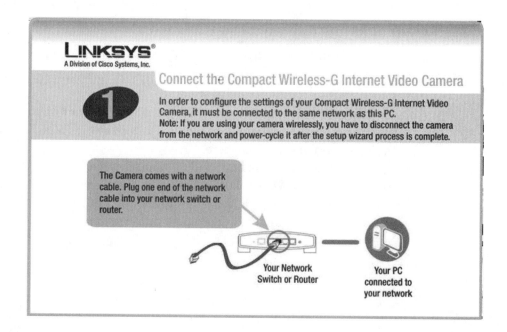

Next, connect the camera to its AC adapter. The camera's blue light will blink for a few seconds and then become steadily illuminated (see Figure 17-3). Click *Next*.

Figure 17-3

Wait for a steady blue light.

Step 3: Find the Address

Once the router has detected the camera, click *Next*. The software will automatically assign the camera a static IP address of 192.168.1.115. On the off chance that this address is already in use by another device on your network, you can change it or have the network automatically assign the camera a new one. You can select either option on the camera's configuration menu; just type the camera's IP address into any browser window, select the Basic menu, and choose a configuration type from the drop-down list (see Figure 17-4).

We'll have the network automatically assign our camera an IP address by selecting *DHCP* from the drop-down list.

Step 4: Enter Today's Date

Now the software will ask you to confirm the camera's name, as well as the date and time, so that it can accurately time-stamp your video (see Figure 17-5). We recommend that you name the camera after the room you'll put it in (in case you end up using more than one).

Figure 17-4

Choose your IP style.

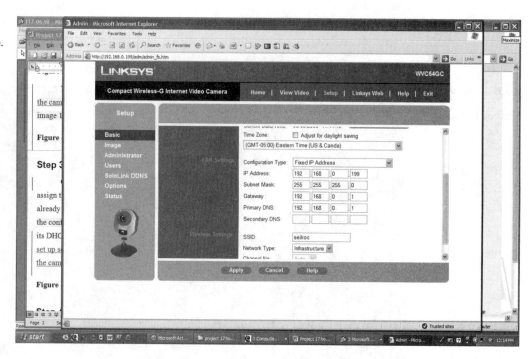

Figure 17-5

Room, date, and time, please.

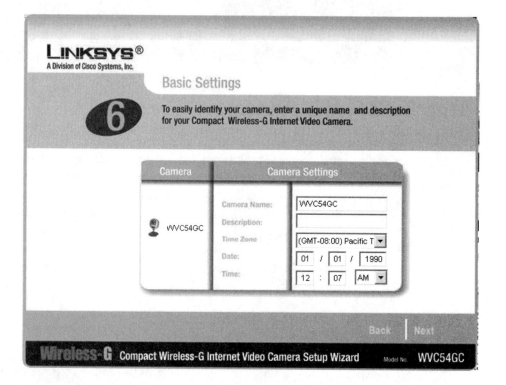

Step 5: Hand Over the Keys

Now it's time to adjust the camera's security settings; enter the network's security type and encryption key (see Figure 17-6) so that it can get online.

Figure 17-6

Plug in the network's
security info.

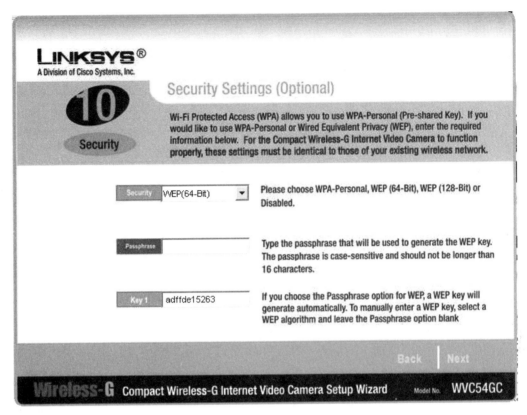

On the following screen, carefully confirm your information (see Figure 17-7)—a small typo or mistake will mean your camera won't connect and you'll have to start all over again.

Step 6: Find More Software

Now, install the Viewer and Recorder Utility, located on the CD that came with the camera. Once it's installed, launch it.

Step 7: Leap into Action!

Now we can test the camera. In the main window of the Viewer and Recorder Utility, click the plus (+) icon to add your camera. The software will search the network for the camera. When it finds yours, select *Add* (see Figure 17-8).

Drag the camera name from the Camera Status window on the left into one of the four viewing windows (see Figure 17-9). Your camera should now be sending a live video feed.

note   *The software can accommodate up to six video feeds at once, which means that you could put a camera in every room in your house and keep an eye on everything from one browser window.*

Figure 17-7

When you're done, double-check you've got it right.

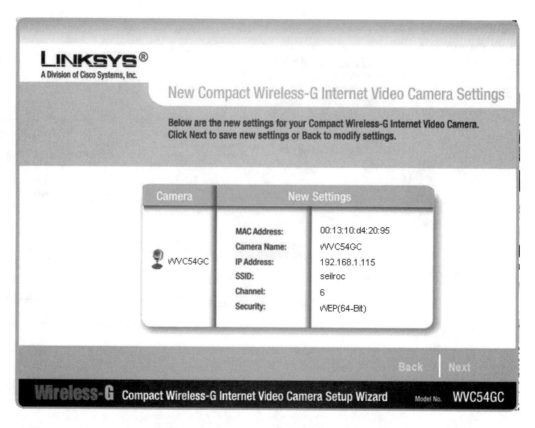

Figure 17-8

Camera found.

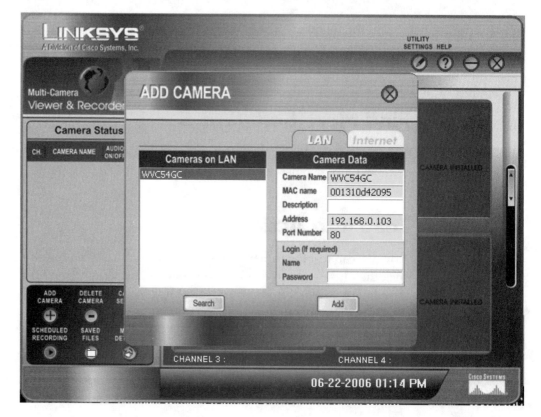

Figure 17-9

Smile, you're on wireless camera.

Step 8: Cut the Cord

With the camera now broadcasting wirelessly, it's time to unplug it from the router. Once disconnected, it should continue broadcasting the live video feed. If it freezes up or stops, restart the router and the Viewer and Recorder software.

Step 9: Try Out SoloLink

Now we'll set the camera to broadcast your video to the Internet—not so that other people can watch your live video feed (for that, check out Project 8), but so that *you* can access your surveillance system from any computer with an Internet connection.

The camera comes with a 3-month trial of Linksys' SoloLink service, which hosts your video feed. The SoloLink software is included on the Linksys CD; install it and launch it. Then click *Next* to have the program search for your camera (see Figure 17-10).

Step 10: Give Up the Codes

Once the camera is detected, you'll need to tell SoloLink your name and password, which are both set to "admin" out of the box (see Figure 17-11).

Figure 17-10

The software searches the network for the camera.

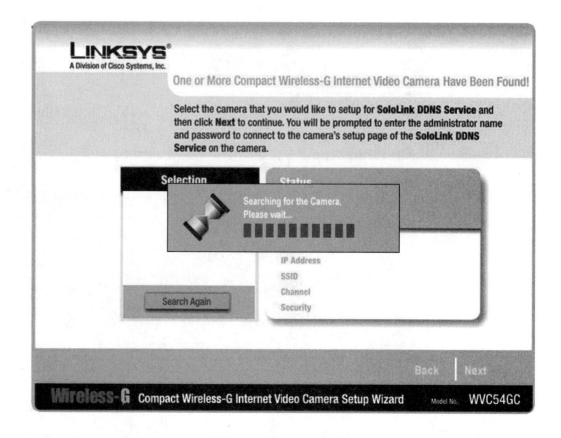

Figure 17-11

Enter the default password to proceed.

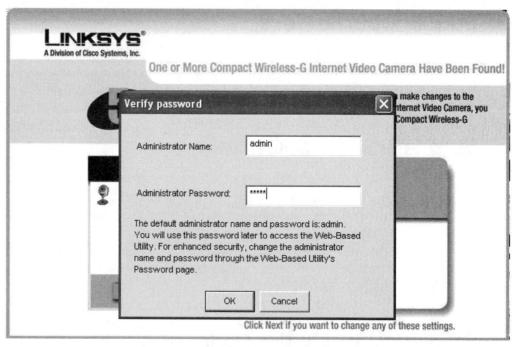

> **tip** *"Admin" isn't much of a name or password; we recommend that you change them to something more secure. To do this, type your camera's IP address into a web browser, and then choose* Setup | Administrator. *Choose any name and a password that's at least 8 characters long.*

To take advantage of the free hosting trial, you'll need to enter the code that's printed on the card that came with the camera (see Figure 17-12).

Figure 17-12

Plug in the code for free hosting.

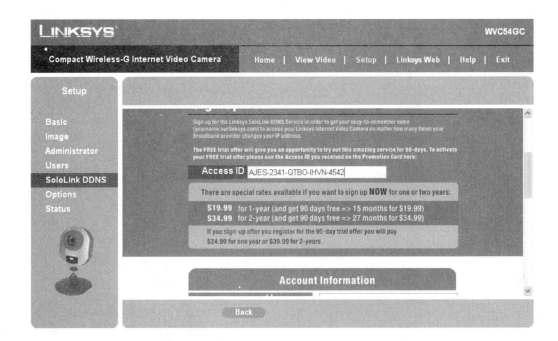

Step 11: License and Registration

Before you can go any further, you'll be required to register with Linksys. Set up an account, and then make sure your web browser can accept cookies—or the process won't work.

tip *To set Internet Explorer to accept cookies, go to Tools | Privacy. Set the security level to Low.*

Choose a name and password and then fill in required personal information. Click *Continue*, and then assign your camera a name. When you're finished pretending to read through the software license, click to accept it.

Now the SoloLink software will assign a web URL to your camera; they'll also send you the URL in a confirmation e-mail. It'll be kind of an odd address, so we suggest that you save the e-mail and bookmark the URL.

Step 12: Set Your Ports

To broadcast your live video feed to the Internet, you'll need to configure your router to use a networking port. For our own particular Linksys router, it's port number 1024; other routers may use a different port, a virtual port, or virtual server. Refer to your router's manual for more information on this.

Step 13: Locate the Camera

Now it's time to put your camera in an inconspicuous location (see Figure 17-13). Though the camera doesn't need to be physically connected to the network, it does need electricity, so you'll need to pick a place near an outlet.

Figure 17-13

No one will ever notice…

note *Find a high area that's unobstructed by stone, brick, or heavy plaster walls. Choice locations may include a high shelf of a bookcase or on a mantle.*

Step 14: Start the Spying

There are two easy ways to get a feed of whatever your camera's filming. Though you can use Linksys's Viewer and Recorder software, you can also simply type the camera's IP address into any web browser—on any PC—and click on *View Video* (see Figure 17-14).

tip *You can zoom in on the action by clicking on the window's magnifying glass icon (see Figure 17-15) and invert the image by clicking the arrow icon.*

Step 15: Let's Go to the Videotape

Of course, you don't have to sit there and watch the video feed in real time; who has time for that? Your camera can actually *record* the video feed, as long as you have the hard drive space to store the video.

Figure 17-14

Instant surveillance, from any PC.

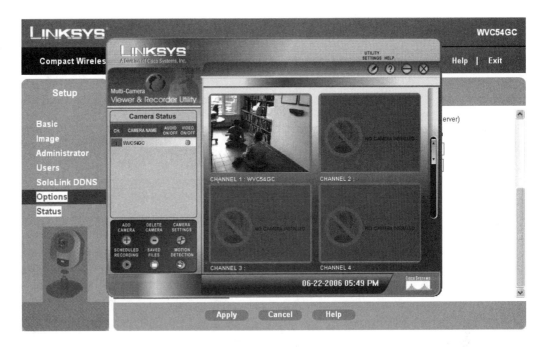

Figure 17-15

Zoom in to catch the details.

To set your camera to record, open up the Viewer and Recorder software and click on *Utility Settings* in the upper right; from here you can tell the camera where to store the video and how much space to allot to it, so as not to max out your hard drive (see Figure 17-16).

Figure 17-16

Don't just watch it—record your surveillance video.

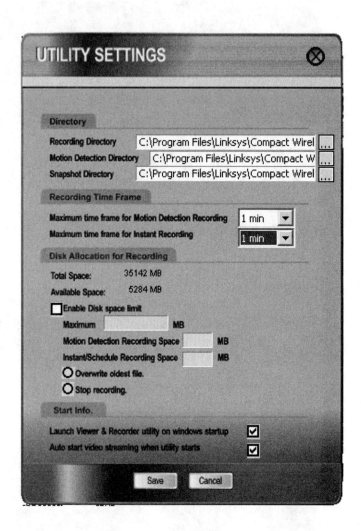

> **tip** *Of course, you can manually select to start recording. In the camera view window, click the red circle in the lower-left corner to begin recording (see Figure 17-17).*

Step 16: Set a Virtual Tripwire

One of the most useful surveillance features is the motion detector, which allows you to start recording only when something moves in the camera's vantage. If you're on vacation or at work, and something moves in front of the camera, it will record a short clip of the action. Color us paranoid, but a short video clip of the action could make the difference in a police investigation.

Figure 17-17

Hit the red button to record.

In the Viewer and Recorder window, click on the *Motion Detection* button. That will open up a configuration menu where you can set parameters on sensitivity and duration (see Figure 17-18). You'll need to try out different settings to find what works for your home; set with too high a sensitivity level, and a change in lighting will trigger the motion detector.

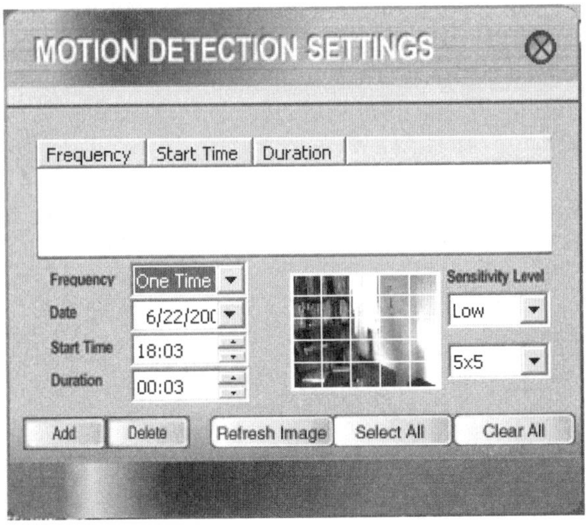

Figure 17-18

Set your camera to record only when there's something worth recording.

> **tip** *If you set up the camera as a surveillance tool when you're not at home, we suggest turning off the blue LED that shows that the camera is live. To do this, access the camera's main configuration settings by typing its IP address into a browser window; then select* Setup | Basic.

Step 17: Set Up Emergency Notification

Now we'll set the software to e-mail you if the camera detects any suspicious movement. In the main configuration window, click on *Options* (see Figure 17-19). Enable the e-mail alert and enter your e-mail address and e-mail account details.

Figure 17-19

An e-mail alert can be sent out when motion is detected.

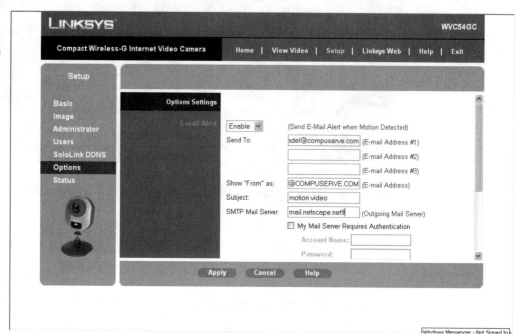

Now, you can rest assured, knowing that wherever you are, you can keep an eye on which is most important to you.

Sync Your Laptop and Your Desktop PC

What You'll Need

- Hardware: Desktop PC, network (wired or wireless) or USB hub
- Software: Microsoft SyncToy
- Cost: Free

These days, many folks have more than one computer, which is a good thing—in theory. But if you work regularly on two computers—a laptop at work and a desktop PC at home, for example—you know that it gets confusing. You end up constantly e-mailing files between the two computers, wondering where you saved something and which version is the most up-to-date. Or maybe your work files are stuck on your laptop, but you prefer to use your desktop PC when you're at home.

Fortunately, it's possible to synchronize two computers so that no matter which one you're using, you're always working with the most recent versions of your data and files. Windows has some basic synchronization functions built in, but they're very limited. Fortunately, Microsoft, generous as it is, offers a more robust utility, called SyncToy, for free on its Web site. While many sync programs take files from one PC and simply replicate them on another, SyncToy works both ways, ensuring that both computers are up to date. So, on Friday afternoon, you can sync your laptop with your desktop PC, work on your desktop PC all weekend, and on Monday morning, go back to your laptop. (By the way, you should take a vacation.)

It's not as if you have to copy everything from your desktop PC onto your laptop, however. You can pick and choose exactly which files and data you want to synchronize, when to do it, and where the files go; the software will even create directories, rename files, and delete older versions of the files.

Now, let's get synced.

Step 1: Round Up the Software

First, you need to download Microsoft's SyncToy application. You can find it on Microsoft's download site at http://www.microsoft.com/downloads/. (You may need to validate that you're working on a genuine—that is, not pirated—version of Windows before you can download the software). Take note that before you install SyncToy, you'll also need to have the Microsoft .NET Framework installed; if you do, skip ahead to Step 2. If your laptop doesn't already have it, when you try to install SyncToy, you'll see this warning message (see Figure 18-1).

Figure 18-1

Before you can use SyncToy, you need the Microsoft .NET Framework.

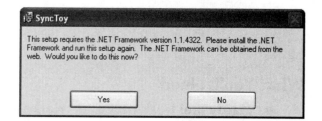

Don't click yes! Rather, click *No*. All you really need is one file, called *dotnetfx .exe*; go back to Microsoft's download site, and search for *.net Redistributable Package*. Download it, double-click it, and install it (see Figure 18-2); it's not small, so this might take a few minutes.

Figure 18-2

Find the dotnetfx.exe file, download it, and click *Run*.

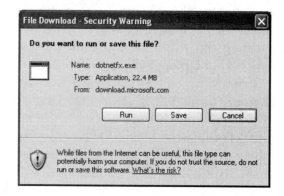

Step 2: Set Up to Sync

Once you've installed the .NET framework software, you're ready to install SyncToy (as outlined in Step 1). Double-click the installation file, and when the wizard comes up, click *Next* (see Figure 18-3), and then go ahead and accept the license terms.

Your first choice is whether to restrict or share it. If you're paranoid by nature, or lots of people use your computer, you might want to restrict access; otherwise, select *Everyone* and click *Next*, and then *Next* again to install the software. When it's finished, click *Close*. If it doesn't come up automatically, open the SyncToy application by clicking the *Start* button | *All Programs* and clicking *SyncToy*.

In the days of old, you had to physically connect two computers to sync them up, but now you can do it over a network—wired or wireless—which makes the whole process easier, faster, and more palatable. SyncToy works by setting up folder pairs—two identical folders, one on your laptop and another on your desktop PC. Once these are set up, SyncToy will move files between them according to the rules you set. When all is said and done, you'll have one folder that's mirrored on two computers.

Step 3: Get Ready to Network

Before we go any further, you need to make sure that both computers are connected to the same local access network (LAN). It can be a wireless or Ethernet-based LAN.

 If you don't already have a home network set up, you can create a virtual one with an inexpensive LAN switch or LAN hub. Just plug both computers into it and it'll create a mini-LAN perfect for synching purposes.

Step 4: Create a Folder Pair

Now, click the button that says *Create New Folder Pair*. We'll create a location for the *Left Folder* on our laptop; click *Browse*, navigate to the My Documents folder on the desktop PC, click *Make New Folder*, and label it *To Sync*. Click *Next*. Now do the same for the *Right Folder* on your desktop PC.

 A network drive is just as good as a PC for sending or receiving files using SyncToy. In fact, you can even use a networked digital camera or music player as a source or destination.

Step 5: Synchronize Everything But the Kitchen Sync

There are many different ways to synchronize your files, each with a slightly different purpose. Here's a quick breakdown of your options:

- **Synchronize:** Moves new and recently changed files back and forth so that you end up with identical files on both machines with duplicate files renamed or deleted.

- **Echo:** Copies recently created or updated files from left to right—that is, from the laptop to the desktop PC—and will delete duplicate items to make this complete. This might work best for those who use their notebook only for creating documents but need the documents on the host PC.

- **Subscribe:** Copies files that are new and updated on the right and moves them to the left, from desktop PC to the laptop. You might want to use this scheme if the desktop periodically gets data or updates files that you need on the notebook, such as in an office.

- **Contribute:** Moves new and updated files from left to right, but won't perform any deletions. This scheme might be good for those who work on their notebooks a lot but don't want the originals on the host PC to be deleted.

- **Combine:** Copies new and updated files in both directions, but won't rename or delete anything. At the cost of having too many files, this synching method is failsafe because nothing is deleted.

Being nervous types, we generally use *Combine*, because nothing gets deleted; that said, as a method, it uses the most hard drive space of the five (see Figure 18-3).

Figure 18-3

We use the Combine option.

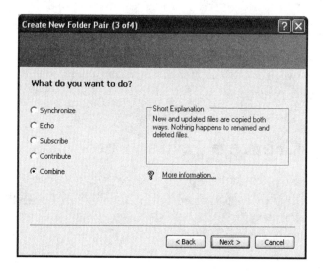

Step 6: Preview Your Setup

Before you let the files fly, try out a Preview. This sets up all the files and goes through a dry run without actually moving any data (see Figure 18-4).

Step 7: Get Ready to Run

After you click Run, the files will fly (see Figure 18-5). Along the way, the file movements are logged and every change will be recorded: successes, failures, directory changes, and so on.

note   *Synching up takes time, especially if you're sending the files over a wireless network. It can take half an hour to synchronize 750 MB of data.*

When the sync is complete, you'll see a summary of all actions (see Figure 18-6).

Figure 18-4

Preview before going whole hog.

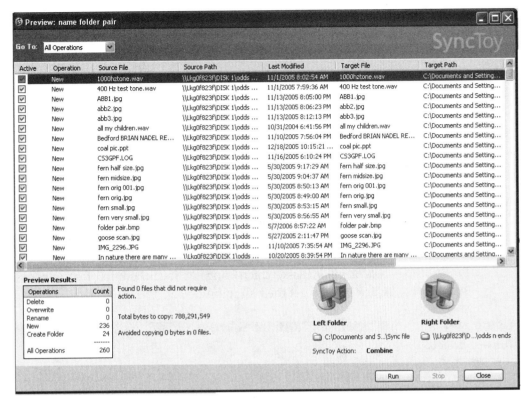

Figure 18-5

Files fly between designated folders.

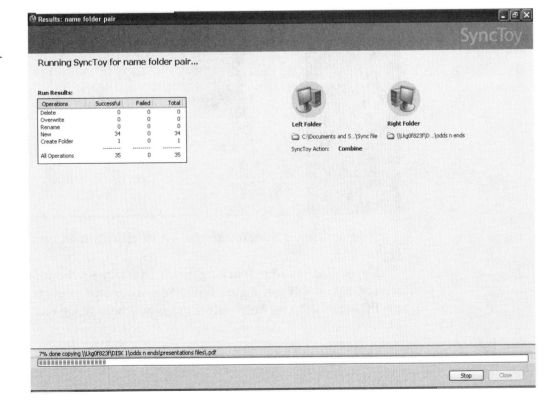

Figure 18-6

What happened?

Operations	Successful	Failed	Total
Delete	0	0	0
Overwrite	0	0	0
Rename	0	0	0
New	167	0	167
Create Folder	18	0	18
	----------	----------	----------
All Operations	185	0	185

Set Up Auto-Sync

SyncToy doesn't have a built-in scheduling function, so if you want to set it up to sync automatically, you'll have to use the one built into Windows XP. Click *Start | All Programs | Accessories | System Tools | Scheduled Tasks*. Now select *Add Scheduled Task*, which brings up the Scheduled Task wizard (see Figure 18-7). Click *Next* to get the ball rolling.

Figure 18-7

This wizard sets up scheduled tasks.

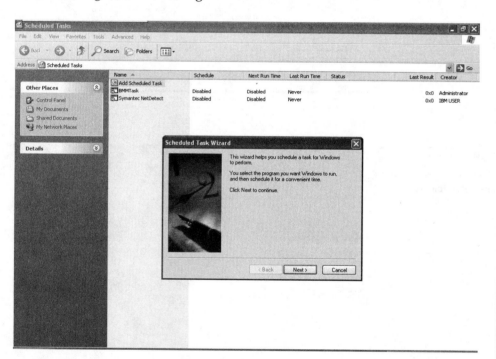

Find and select SyncToy in the list of applications, and click *Next* (see Figure 18-8).

Depending on your synching needs, you can set the utility to run daily, weekly, or monthly (see Figure 18-9). We use our laptop at work and our desktop PC at home, so we keep ours set to sync when we log on.

Figure 18-8

Click to highlight
SyncToy.

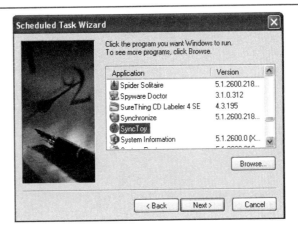

Figure 18-9

Choose how often.

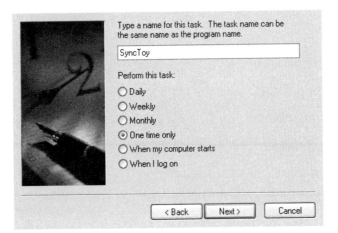

Next, set the time for synchronization. If you protect your PC with a password, you'll have to enter it here to ensure that the transfer goes smoothly. After reviewing the confirmation screen, click *Finish*.

Project 19

Clean Up Your Notebook

What You'll Need

- Hardware: Flashlight, can of compressed air, microfiber cloth, small Phillips-head screwdriver, glass cleaner, and lint-free wipes
- Software: Microsoft Windows
- Cost: Free to $50 U.S.

You wear clean clothes, you brush your teeth after every meal, and your desk is neat and tidy with all the pencils lined up next to one another. So why does your laptop look like you've used it as a plate for a Big Mac? We know the scene: the screen is caked with the accumulated grime of years of use, the keyboard is awash in a sea of crumbs, and that's just the stuff you can see—don't even think about all the dust balls and dirt that's gotten inside. Laptops don't clean themselves and yours will require periodic maintenance—inside and out—to live a long and healthy life. In this chapter, we'll show you how to get inside and clean the guts of your laptop, and how to keep it looking spiffy on the outside, too.

Step 1: Keep Your Cool

Computer components—processors, graphics cards, and the like—get hot when they run. That's all well and good for a big desktop PC, where the components have lots of room to breathe and cool off. But in your laptop, they're all packed together, like sardines in a can, and if it gets too hot in there, your components—and your laptop—will fry. To mitigate this, laptop makers put in elaborate *heat sinks* that absorb the heat generated by the processor. In addition, all but the tiniest models have at least a single fan; some bigger systems have two or even three. When the temperature rises above a certain level, the fans automatically come on to keep the laptop out of the red zone. Unfortunately, like all fans, the ones in your laptop will eventually end up covered in dust and dirt, and that could spell trouble.

See a CNET video on cleaning up your laptop computer at http://diylaptop.cnet.com

An occasional cleaning will keep your laptop fans spinning effectively for years. But before you can clean them, you'll have to find them first. Fortunately, in most cases, they're near the vents that are located around the edges of your case; these slats let cool air in and hot air out. Don't worry if they're covered in dust and lint—we'll get to that. Now you'll need to open up the laptop case.

Look for a few sets of screws, underneath the laptop, near the vents. Remove the panel (see Figure 19-1), and look for the fans—they're circular and plastic, usually about the size of a quarter, with a small propeller inside. Again, they may be covered with dust and lint.

Figure 19-1

Open the machine for inspection.

tip   *Put all the panels and tiny screws (see Figure 19-2) into a box or plastic bag for safekeeping. There's nothing worse than doing a great cleanup and then not being able to put your laptop back together because you lost a part.*

Step 2: Kick Out the Dust Bunnies

Now that you're inside the laptop, use a flashlight to look around for built-up dust and dirt. Using the eraser-end of a pencil or a tweezer, pick off any nasty deposits you come across (see Figure 19-3).

Start at the fan and work your way to the ducts and vents. Look under the ribbon cables, around the hard drive, and near the tiny circuit boards. Grime can hide in the oddest places, like the processor's copper-colored heat sink, so make sure you explore all the laptop's nooks and crannies.

Figure 19-2

Put all the parts in a safe place while working.

Figure 19-3

A pencil's eraser is a great probe for inspecting a notebook.

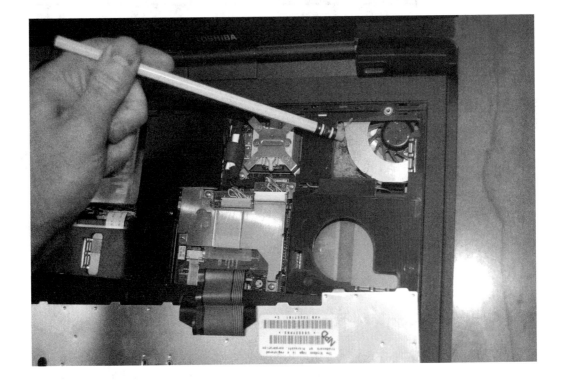

note *Look at the processor, RAM, and hard drive. Are they scorched? Are their labels peeling off? These are the telltale signs of a machine that has overheated. If the contacts look burnt or you've been having problems with the notebook shutting down prematurely, consider replacing any burnt parts. At the very least, you'll need to take extra caution to keep the air flowing within and around your laptop. Make sure that none of the vents are blocked. And you may want to shell out for a USB-powered cooling base, which will blow cool air into the notebook. They cost about $25.*

Step 3: Air It All Out

You've done the detail work, and now it's time to go big. Put on a dust mask, if you have one. Grab the can of compressed air and spray down the inside of your laptop (see Figure 19-4). Go nuts. Blow out all the dust you can find. It won't be pretty, and you might want to have a vacuum cleaner running nearby to grab all the junk it as it comes out. Don't be surprised if a lot comes out of that little laptop.

Figure 19-4

Blow out everything that isn't tied down.

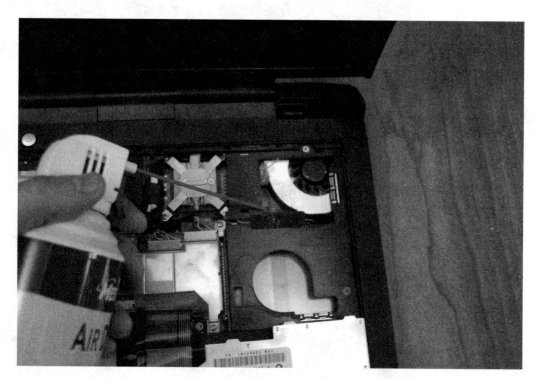

Step 4: Shake, Rattle, and Roll

Now that you've made your first pass at cleaning out the inside, give your laptop a little shake to dislodge any particularly resilient dust and grime. Keep cleaning and shaking until nothing more comes out.

tip *If you have a squeaky fan, this is the time to fix it, and a little oil should do the trick. Spray a tiny amount of WD-40 (or another lubricant) onto a cotton swab and apply it to the center of the fan (see Figure 19-5). If this doesn't help, replace the entire fan. It's easy to do: most are held down by two or three screws and have a basic snap-apart electrical connection. Many electronics stores stock replacement fans.*

Figure 19-5

The squeaky fan gets the grease.

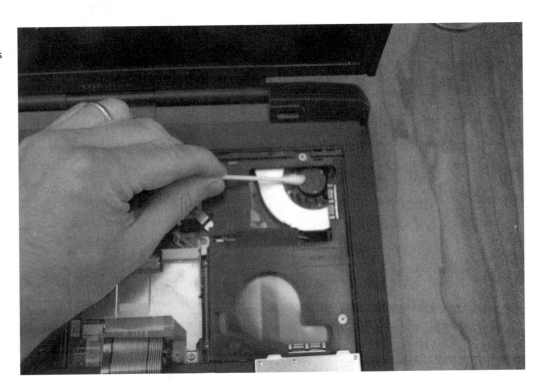

Step 5: Clean Up the Crumb Highway

Now that the inside of your laptop is as clean as a whistle, it's time to tidy up that nasty keyboard. Don't be embarrassed: most keyboards have enough crumbs to feed a flock of diseased pigeons for weeks. Use the can of compressed air to blow it clean (see Figure 19-6), but be careful not to break off any keys.

tip *If you get a bit too overzealous while cleaning and break a key off the keyboard, try using Super Glue to stick it back on. If that doesn't work, you can replace the whole kit and caboodle. First you'll need to take the old one off; most have screws that are covered by a piece of trim, while others require you to pry them loose. If the approach is not obvious, consult the manufacturer's web site or call tech support. Once you've got the keyboard out, disconnect the data line. (And hang on to that old keyboard—you might need some replacement keys one day.) Next, connect the new keyboard's data ribbon and snap it all back into place before restarting the machine. The entire procedure shouldn't take more than a few minutes. The Spare Parts Warehouse (www.sparepartswarehouse.com) stocks replacement keyboards for most major laptop models.*

Figure 19-6

Aim between the keys.

Step 6: Tighten Up

While you've still got the laptop open, give each of the major components a quick look to see if any are loose. A loose motherboard or hard drive can cause damage in the long run, so make sure all of the screws are tight, and that all of the cables are well connected. When tightening the screws, be careful not to overdo it—gently tighten until you feel some resistance. When you're done, reconnect the access panels on the underside of your laptop.

note   *Did anything mysterious fall out of your laptop while you were cleaning it? Maybe a few screws, a bit of plastic, some metal filings—perhaps even an odd bug or two? Don't worry, this is common; just make sure all of the components are securely connected before you close up the laptop for good.*

Step 7: Clean Your Screen

All laptop screens are susceptible to nicks and scratches, and the latest glossy, high-contrast displays show off fingerprints that even Columbo couldn't miss. We like to give our screens a quick rubdown about once a week. You can use any brand of window cleaner so long as it doesn't contain ammonia or any harsh detergents. We're partial to Sprayway, because it gets all foamy and doesn't leave annoying streaks (see Figure 19-7); if you can't find it at your local supermarket or hardware store, try drugstore.com.

Figure 19-7

Spray down and wipe clean.

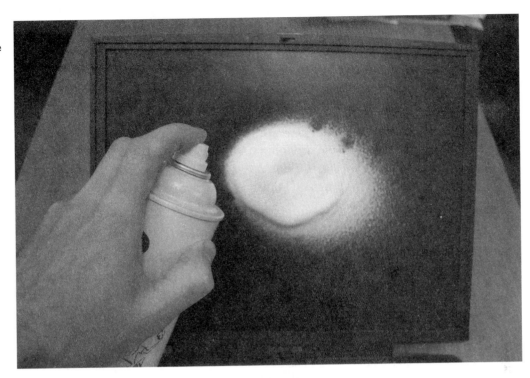

When wiping down the screen, stay away from tissues, which will leave lint behind, and rough fabrics that may scratch the display. We recommend Kimwipes lint-free cleaning cloths or a soft cotton shammy or a microfiber cloth (see Figure 19-8).

Figure 19-8

Clear off dust with a microfiber cloth.

Between serious cleanings, dust and fingerprints on the display can be easily removed with a soft microfiber cloth. Make circles across the display, and wipe toward one edge of the display.

Step 8: Get a Bag for Safety

Laptops are delicate things, and every time you take yours out into the world, you run the risk of damaging it. A good bag is your laptop's best friend when you're away from home base. There are a ton of laptop bags on the market; you'll want one with lots of padding and enough pockets for all of your accessories. Whether it's a messenger bag, a backpack, or a traditional briefcase design, find something that can protect your baby and use it.

tip *If your laptop's case does crack or break, it'll probably be prohibitively expensive, if not plain impossible, to replace it. However, small cracks or breaks can be fixed with silicone sealant. It's not the most elegant solution, but it will work. Larger cracks and holes, on the other hand, can be filled easily with plumber's epoxy putty. Epoxy usually comes in two tubes; you blend the two substances together, press the resulting putty into the hole, and smooth it out with a plasterers' knife. After a few minutes, the putty will harden. If it looks ugly, you can use some fine sandpaper to blend it into the case, and then paint it to match. Personally, we'd leave it au naturel and let it stand as our DIY badge of honor.*

Laptop Day Spa

How your laptop looks on the outside is important, yes, but how healthy it is on the inside is critical. So treat your laptop to a digital day spa. It'll only take an hour or two, and you don't even have to be around for most of that time. Start by cleaning the hard drive of digital detritus with Windows' error-checking routine, which goes through the drive a sector at a time looking for, and correcting, data placement errors. Open Windows Explorer, right-click on the hard drive, and select *Properties*. Now click on the *Tools* tab and then *Check Now*. Check both boxes—to automatically fix errors and recover bad sectors—and let the machine do its thing. Note that you may need to first restart the machine, if prompted.

Next we'll *defragment* the hard drive, physically reorganizing its contents in order to store the pieces of each file close together and in order. This should make your laptop run smoother and maybe even start up quicker. In that same Windows Explorer dialog box, click on the *Defragment Now* box. Once the interface comes up, click *Defragment*. This process can take an hour or so for a drive that's been around the block, so set it and forget it (see Figure 19-9).

One more tip for good hard drive health. Internet Explorer can be a hard drive hog, and will eat up gigabytes of unnecessary data if you let it. To keep

Figure 19-9

Defrag the drive to make it run smoothly.

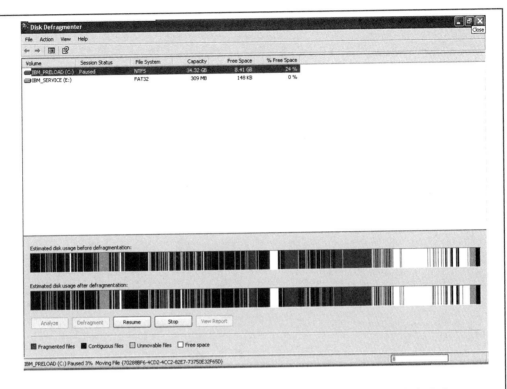

IE in its place, open Internet Explorer, select the *Tools* menu, and click *Internet Options*. In the *Temporary Internet files* box, click *Settings*. Move the slider to set the amount of space you want to devote to IE (see Figure 19-10); we set ours to 5000 MB (which equals 5 GB), which should be more than enough.

Figure 19-10

Adjust how much space IE takes up.

Squeeze More Life out of Your Battery

What You'll Need

- Hardware: Spare battery (optional)
- Software: Battery-monitoring program (optional)
- Cost: Free to $50 U.S.

It is a truth universally acknowledged that a laptop's battery never lasts long enough. Whether you're in the middle of working on a presentation during a cross-country flight or watching the final scene of *Citizen Kane*, there's never a convenient time for the battery to conk out. Despite impressive gains in battery chemistry and packaging, and new, low-voltage components that sip power instead of gulp it, the average laptop still runs for only about 3 hours per charge.

Whether you're working, or playing, or both, making a few adjustments to your laptop can squeeze an additional hour or two out of the battery. In this chapter, we'll show you how to hone your power management settings, take better care of your battery's cells, and turn off unneeded components—all of which will help keep your laptop running longer.

note *Each of your laptop's components—the processor, RAM, hard drive, and graphics card—draw power from the battery. As a general rule, the faster and more powerful the components, the more juice they require. A high-end, speedy processor and hard drive will make your laptop run faster, but they'll also drain your battery more quickly than their mid-range and low-end counterparts. On the other hand, adding extra RAM (Project 22) may deliver a significant (and cost-effective) performance boost without sacrificing much battery life.*

Step 1: Manage Your Power

The quickest route to better battery life is by tweaking Windows XP's built-in power management settings. To access these settings, click on the *Start* button in the lower-left corner of your screen, select *Control Panel*, and double-click the *Power Options* icon.

Within the *Power Schemes* tab in the Power Options Properties dialog box, you'll notice a drop-down box labeled *Power schemes* (see Figure 20-1). These preset profiles, which range from *Always On* to *Max Battery*, modify when (and if) your laptop turns off the display and hard disk and initiates Standby mode. If you're trying to get as many minutes out of the battery as possible, set the scheme to *Max Battery*. Note that you can also fine-tune the individual settings and save your own handmade profiles.

Figure 20-1

Windows power schemes let you optimize for better battery life.

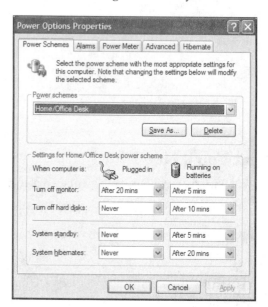

tip   *It's a good idea to check your laptop manufacturer's web site for a new version of your model's firmware—that is, the software embedded in the hardware—every few months. Firmware updates often contain an update of the BIOS—short for basic input and output system—which controls many of your computer's operational parameters. Among other things, manufacturers often add power-saving features to the BIOS that can extend a laptop's run time. Often, if you register your laptop on the manufacturer's web site, they'll notify you when a new firmware update is available.*

It will take some time to find the right settings, and you may want to design several power schemes tailored to the things you do most. If you're surfing the Web at a coffee shop, you'll want different settings than if you're watching a DVD at home. Conveniently, you can maintain separate settings for when the laptop is plugged in and when it's running on batteries (see Figure 20-2). To get you started, try out our "Chilling at Starbucks" scheme wherein the monitor turns off after 5 minutes, the hard drive shuts down after 10 minutes, and the system hibernates after 15 minutes.

tip   *Believe it or not, a screensaver can cut 10 minutes or more from your battery life by using the screen when it isn't needed. To maximize your battery life, set the screensaver to Blank in the* Display Properties *dialog box (accessible by right-clicking on the Desktop, and selecting* Properties*).*

Figure 20-2

You can dictate exactly when each component shuts down.

Step 2: Know Your Battery

So that you always have an accurate idea of how much battery life you have left, we recommend that you set your laptop to display the battery's charge level in the *taskbar*—that little strip or tray of tiny icons that runs along the bottom right of the Windows desktop. Just hover the cursor over the battery symbol (or the plug symbol, if your laptop is plugged in) and it will report what percentage of the battery remains (see Figure 20-3). It will also give you an (notoriously unreliable) estimate of how much battery time you have left.

Figure 20-3

Mousing over the battery icon shows you how much power remains.

 If you travel regularly with your laptop, it's a good idea to have a second battery on hand, charged and ready to go. Most spare batteries weigh a pound or less and could make the difference between finding out how the movie ends or finishing that career-making memo. There are also high-capacity battery packs that can run for as much as twice as long as the one that came with your laptop.

Step 3: Be Alarmed... Very Alarmed

Unless you're keeping a very close eye on your battery, it may die and catch you by surprise. And trust us: It makes for a bad (and sad) time if your laptop shuts down before you have a chance to save whatever you're working on. Fortunately, you can avert disaster by setting your laptop's battery alarms. There are two of them—one to let you know when your battery has reached a low level and another to alert you when your laptop is about to go totally dead. To set the alarms, go to the *Alarms* tab in the Power Options Properties dialog box (see Figure 20-4). We recommend setting the *Low battery alarm* to 5 percent and the *Critical battery alarm* to 3 percent. If you're particularly nervous, and want even more advance warning, go ahead and set these levels higher.

Figure 20-4

Get a warning before your battery runs out.

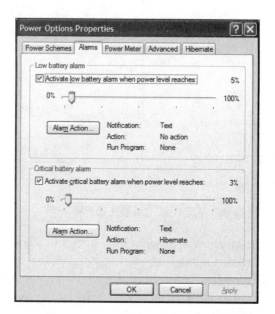

> **tip**   *For a more personalized touch, you can set exactly how your laptop will warn you about a dying battery. On the Alarms tab, select the* Alarm Action *button. From there, you can choose whether it sounds an actual alarm or pops up a text message. For those who wear a belt and suspenders, you can set it to use both audio and visual alarms. You can also set the laptop to automatically go to sleep or turn off.*

Step 4: Give Your Laptop Some Rest

Bears do it. Drunks do it. You do it. So why not let your laptop go to sleep—when you're not using it. There are a few ways to cut back on battery power without actually turning your laptop off. First, you can put it into Standby mode by clicking the *Start* button, selecting *Turn Off Computer*, and clicking *Standby*. In this state, the contents of the hard drive are saved only temporarily. We prefer the *Hibernation* feature, which saves all of the data you're working with onto a special section of the hard drive; when you start up again, you can pick up exactly where you left off. To turn this feature on, select the *Hibernate* tab in the Power Options Properties dialog box (see Figure 20-5), and click *Enable Hibernation*. Windows automatically calculates how much space is needed for successful hibernation, so make sure you've got at least that amount of room available on your hard drive.

Figure 20-5

When there's nothing left to do, let your laptop hibernate.

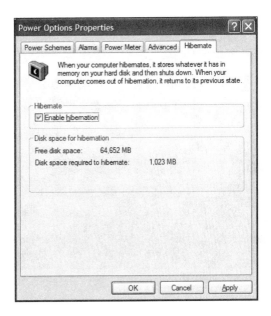

> tip
>
> *Travelers who use a laptop are always keeping an eye open for a good place to get a charge. A special car cigarette lighter adapter will charge your battery while you drive. AC adapters are often hidden in airport lounges, office lobbies, and coffee shops. Intercity trains, like Amtrak's Acela and Metroliner, sometimes have outlets built into the seats. In a tight spot, on a plane, you can use the airplane lavatory's outlet, though you run the risk of starting a riot if you take too long.*

Step 5: Dim the Lights

The display is one of your laptop's biggest power hogs, plain and simple. By adjusting its brightness level to the bare minimum (that you can still see), you can add as much as half an hour of battery life.

> note
>
> *Some newer laptops have an* ambient light sensor, *which automatically adjusts the screen brightness to suit environmental lighting conditions. If you're looking to conserve battery life, we recommend that you set this feature to a maximum brightness of 75 percent—or turn it off entirely.*

Step 6: Cut the Peripherals

Peripherals such as a WiFi radio can eat up valuable battery time, so turn them off when they're not in use. Some laptops have a WiFi power switch, but others may require you to right-click on the wireless networking icon (see Figure 20-6) and disable it. Other power-sucking peripherals include external hard drives and optical drives, PC Cards, and web cams.

Figure 20-6

Not surfing the Web? Turn it off.

> **tip**   *Some devices draw a small but steady amount of power so that they're ready for use. Disconnect any PC Card or USB device to make sure it's not wasting even a little battery life.*

Step 7: Maximize Your Battery's Effectiveness

If you think your laptop battery has a bottomless well of energy, you're wrong. Batteries, which produce electricity as the result of a complex chemical reaction, can be adversely affected by temperature and other trying physical conditions. They also degrade over time. There are some best practices, however, that will help your batteries live long, healthy lives; where most batteries will deliver at least 200 full charge cycles, following these tips can push that to 300 or more.

- Break new cells in gently with three full charge-discharge cycles.
- Never allow a battery to get hotter than 100 degrees or colder than 50 degrees Fahrenheit.
- If your laptop will be plugged in for an extended period, disconnect the battery.
- Periodically clean the contacts on your laptop and battery (Figure 20-7) with alcohol.
- If you notice that it's starting to drain faster, recondition again with three full charge-discharge cycles.

Figure 20-7

Give your battery the
alcohol treatment.

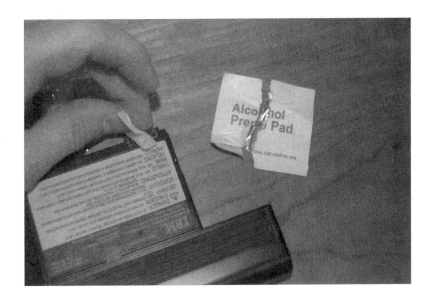

A Battery of Tests

Some manufacturers, such as HP, ship their laptops with utilities that can diagnose problems and even prolong battery life. HP's program, which only works for recent HP models, is free and available at www.hp.com/go/techcenter/battery.

Figure 20-8

The battery doctor
will see you now.

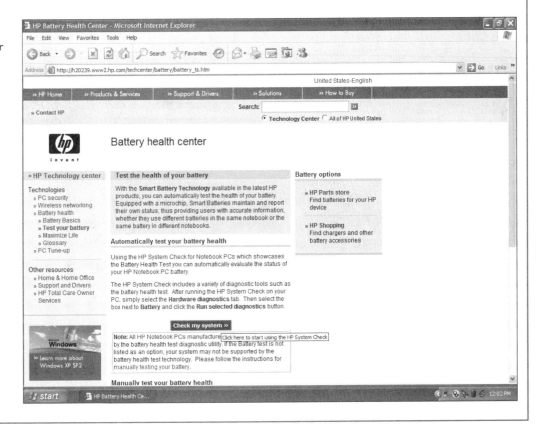

Once you're at the web site, select *Test your battery* (see Figure 20-8), and then click on *Check my system*. The site will install a small application and then give your battery a little checkup (see Figure 20-9). You'll get a report that details any problems your battery might have, what to do about them, and URLs for downloads that might help (see Figure 20-10).

Figure 20-9

The utility gives the battery a workout.

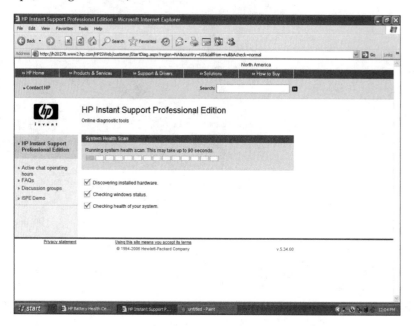

Figure 20-10

The battery report can reveal problems.

Step 8: Wait, There's More!

Regardless of what type of laptop you have, a battery-monitoring program will give you some insight into the health of your laptop. There are a few utilities that will do the trick, but our favorite is BatteryMon, which you can download at www.download .com or www.passmark.com. Go ahead and download the file, and then double-click it to install the program.

Once it's installed, start the program, unplug your laptop, and work as normal. The software will create a graph of the battery's key parameters, which will tell you exactly how much capacity is left (see Figure 20-11). If you periodically run the test, you'll see over time if your battery's capacity is declining.

Figure 20-11

Watch your battery drain.

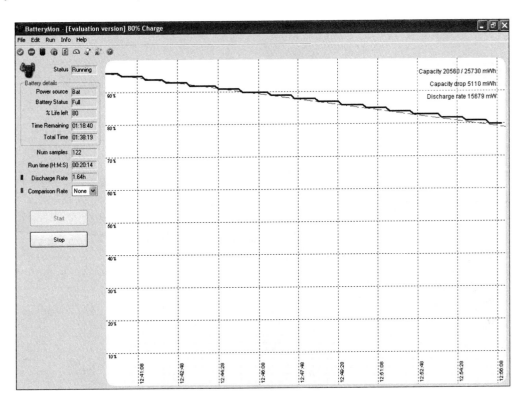

tip *When your battery is no longer holding a full charge, it's time to get rid of it. But after so many years of faithful service, doesn't it deserve a dignified funeral? In addition to lithium, mercury, and other toxic chemicals, batteries are host to a variety of environmentally unfriendly materials and should never be thrown away in the trash. You can bring them into a nearby electronics superstore or a battery recycling station. Look online to find one near you.*

Upgrade Your Operating System

What You'll Need

- Software: Ubuntu
- Cost: Free

Fed up with Windows? Don't want to shell out all that money for a Macintosh? Meet Linux, a free operating system that's arguably more stable and secure—some might say all-around superior—to those peddled by Microsoft and Apple. Originally developed by Finnish university student Linus Torvalds, Linux is open-source software, meaning that it's free and open to developers, thousands of whom have contributed to and improved it since it first appeared in 1991.

On top of being free, Linux has very basic hardware requirements, which makes it capable of injecting new life into an old, tired laptop. To illustrate this point, we'll be using a "vintage" Fujitsu LifeBook S6000 laptop we bought on eBay for $200 with a Pentium III processor, a 30 GB hard drive, and the lousy Windows 98 operating system, which is bogged down and running *slow*. When we're done, it'll run as fast, smoothly, and capably as a new Windows or Mac laptop.

note *Ubuntu's minimum system requirements are about as modest as can be: a laptop with 128 MB of RAM and 1.8 GB of hard drive space.*

Linux does force you to make a few sacrifices, however. You'll have to do without all of those applications that you've grown to love (or hate). That's right: neither Windows nor Mac software runs on Linux. That said, there are tons of free (or inexpensive) Linux applications out there, which are often similar to the ones you're accustomed to; we recommend some of our favorites at the end of this chapter. You may also have trouble finding software drivers for the peripherals you want to hook up, and it may require some legwork to get your Linux laptop to recognize your printer, digital camera, or MP3 player.

There are many different companies that offer Linux packages. Our favorite, Ubuntu, is 100 percent free and compatible with most any laptop out there, whether it uses an Intel, AMD, or PowerPC processor or started out as a Mac or Windows system. Even so, we recommend that you check with your laptop's manufacturer to make sure it's Linux-compatible.

Let's get started.

Step 1: Get Ubuntu

You can either download Ubuntu from the company's web site (www.ubuntu.com) or have them mail the discs to you (see Figure 21-1); they'll even pay the postage!

Figure 21-1

Delivered to your home: Ubuntu installation discs.

note *An African word, Ubuntu means "humanity to others" or "I am what I am because of who we all are," emphasizing the community aspect of open-source software. We're down with that.*

It's not like you'll be getting just an operating system—the Ubuntu package includes the OpenOffice suite of productivity applications, which includes programs for word processing, working with spreadsheets and databases, web browsing, and more. The OpenOffice apps are streamlined and simple to use—a real breath of fresh air compared to the highly complicated applications you've been dealing with. Even better, the OpenOffice applications can read Microsoft Office files (and vice versa), so you'll still be able to work and communicate with the non-Linux world.

Step 2: Load It Up

Like the Windows and Mac operating systems, Linux is a big program. There's a lot of software to load, but once you initiate the installation process, it's mostly automatic.

Step 3: Start the Installation

To start the installation process, press Enter (see Figure 21-2).

Figure 21-2

We want the default installation.

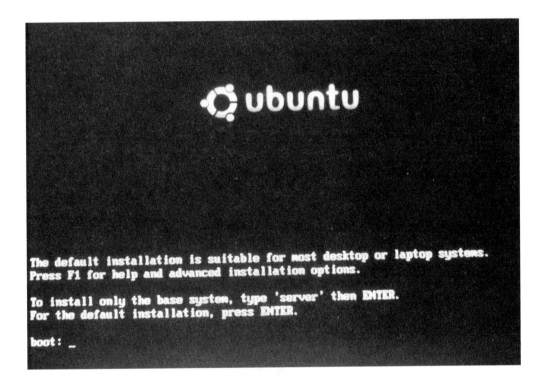

When asked, choose your language and country (see Figure 21-3).

Figure 21-3

Habla Linux?

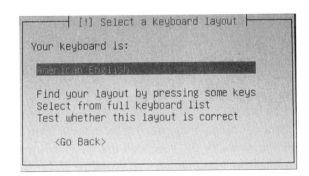

Step 4: Configure Your Hardware

During the installation, Ubuntu will seek out your laptop's hardware. When it has identified what you've got, it will automatically configure the hardware to make sure it runs properly (see Figure 21-4).

Figure 21-4

Hardware detection in progress.

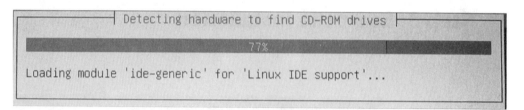

Step 5: Set Up Wireless Networking

Next up is networking. If you connect to a primary wireless network (see Project 2 to learn how to set one up), you'll need to tell Ubuntu your network name and WEP encryption code (see Figure 21-5).

Figure 21-5

You can trust Ubuntu; give up your wireless security code.

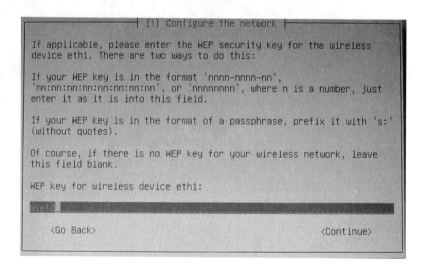

Ubuntu will attempt to connect to your network. If it doesn't work, don't sweat it; you'll be able to change the networking settings later.

Step 6: Name That Host

It's now time to give your Linux system a name; "Ubuntu" is the default setting, but in honor of Ubuntu's generosity, we're going to call ours "Freebook." This name is just for the laptop, however; you'll be picking a name and password for each system user later on.

Step 7: Reformat Your Hard Drive

Ubuntu will now reformat your hard drive using the EXT3 scheme, which is much more efficient than the Windows scheme. It's a quick process—a 40 GB drive will take about 5 minutes (see Figure 21-6). Ubuntu will let you manually partition the drive, so that you can hang on to some of your old data, but that gets fairly complicated. In fact, the easiest way for you to keep your old data is to move it onto an external drive. As for us, we're going to start from scratch and wipe the sucker clean.

Figure 21-6

You can keep your old stuff or start fresh.

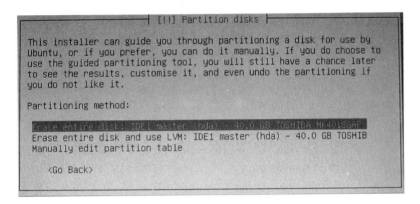

Step 8: Take a Break

The program now does its thing (see Figure 21-7), installing the thousands of files needed to create a modern Linux operating system (and OpenOffice). Our system took about 20 minutes, so you've got time to go make a sandwich.

Figure 21-7

Fifteen minutes—patience is a virtue.

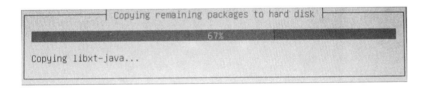

Step 9: The Finishing Touches

After entering your time zone, you'll need to choose a user name and password. Then Ubuntu will restart your system. As it starts up, it checks all of its modules, providing you with some useful diagnostic information (see Figure 21-8); if you ever have trouble starting the system or one part loads slowly, look there to isolate the problem.

Step 10: Welcome to Linux

You'll be relieved to see that there isn't that much of a difference between the Linux desktop and what you're accustomed to. Still, be ready for some slight differences.

Figure 21-8

You get a full diagnostic checkup during startup.

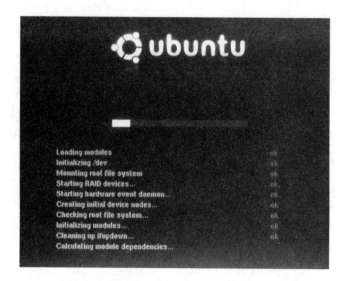

Though we could write a whole book about the ins and outs of Linux, we'll give you a brief orientation.

You'll notice the three icons that sit along the top of the desktop: the globe, which starts the Mozilla Firefox Internet browser; an envelope and clock, which launches the e-mail and calendar application; and the life preserver, which initiates the help utility (see Figure 21-9).

Figure 21-9

Meet your new desktop.

The trash can at the lower right—well, you should know what goes in there. Rather than the taskbar icons that automatically load in Windows, you can choose which items appear in the Panels space along the bottom of the screen.

Step 11: Make Yourself at Home

The File Browser will be familiar to Windows and Mac users. The master folder list sits along the left margin, and individual files and documents are displayed in the main part of the window (see Figure 21-10); you can use the magnifying glass to zoom in and out of them.

Figure 21-10

A familiar friend: the file browser.

Recommended Software for Linux

An operating system is only as good as the software that runs on it. While there's less to choose from than with Windows or the Mac OS, there's a good assortment of Linux programs available—and a lot of it is free.

● **Mozilla Firefox:** One of the best web browsers on the market, Firefox offers greater security and less vulnerability than Internet Explorer, and is included with the Ubuntu package.

- **OpenOffice:** Includes programs for word processing, e-mail, calendaring, working with spreadsheets, and giving presentations, plus a heavy-duty database application. It can export files to Adobe Acrobat format supported by Windows and Mac computers. This suite comes with the Ubuntu package or can be downloaded on its own.

- **Logi.Crypto:** Security application that encrypts the data on your hard drive.

- **GNUCash:** Bears a remarkable similarity to Intuit's Quicken financial software; keeps track of budgets.

- **Games:** Many popular games, such as Doom, are Linux-compatible.

Upgrade Your Memory

What You'll Need

- **Hardware: New RAM module(s), two plastic baggies, pencil**
- **Software: CPU-Z (CPU-ID), RAM Optimizer (AceLogiX)**
- **Cost: $50 to $100 U.S.**

Random access memory. We know; it sounds super geeky. Go ahead—say it in a nerdy voice. Ridiculous. Nevertheless, random access memory, usually called RAM, is perhaps the best-kept secret of computer performance. Though processors and hard drives get most of the attention, upgrading your laptop's RAM is one of the least expensive ways to boost performance—and it won't take a bite out of your battery life, as a faster processor or larger hard drive could.

Best of all, upgrading your RAM is one of the easiest upgrade procedures because the chips are easy to get at, usually located right behind a hatch on the bottom panel of your laptop.

caution *One important caveat: If you have an older laptop, some or all of its RAM may be soldered onto the motherboard; changing that type of RAM requires special expertise and is almost always more trouble than it's worth. If you're unsure whether your RAM is fixed to the motherboard, you'll need to do some research online. Go to your laptop manufacturer's web site to find out what type of motherboard your model uses and if the memory modules are soldered on to it (this information should be listed in the technical specs). Of course, you can just open up the access panel (detailed in Step 2) and see if there are separate RAM modules or not.*

We'll be working on an old laptop that has two 128 MB RAM modules for a paltry total of 256 MB; that might have been enough a few years ago, but it won't keep up with today's applications. So, we'll be quadrupling that to an even 1 GB—what we consider to be the optimal amount for the average user. Even if your laptop already has 512 MB of RAM, an upgrade to 1 GB should result in a noticeable burst of performance speed. And if you've already got 1 GB, well, doubling up to 2 GB should make your laptop a bona fide screamer.

Before you begin this project (or any other that involves opening up your laptop), it's critical that you cleanse yourself of static electricity, which can damage your laptop's delicate circuitry. You can rid yourself of static by touching a cold water pipe or some other large, grounded, metal, non electrical object, or by wearing a grounding bracelet (which you can find at the hardware store). Also, avoid working in a carpeted room.

Step 1: Give Your Memory a Checkup

If you don't already know how much RAM you've got under the hood, the first step is to find out. The best way to do it is with CPU-Z, a free utility available at www. cpuid.com. Download the software, unzip it, and double-click the icon to run the program.

CPU-Z will spit out a lot of information about your laptop's components and performance parameters; for now, we're only interested in the chip speed and other details listed in the Memory tab. In fact, go ahead and print out the screen of diagnostic information on the Memory tab. After the upgrade, we'll run CPU-Z again and compare the old specs to the new. And we'll laugh. Oh, how we'll laugh.

Step 2: Make the First Incision

Shut your laptop down. Unplug it. Take the battery out. Give it a minute or two. Before you open it up, your laptop needs to be fully off; listen to make sure the fans have stopped spinning.

Turn your laptop over, so you're facing the underside. The RAM modules are usually located behind a small panel that's often marked by a microchip icon. Un-screw the panel, put the screws into a plastic baggie (so you don't lose them), and pop the cover off (see Figure 22-1).

Figure 22-1

Remove the panel.

There may be a flexible plastic shield protecting the RAM; go ahead and pull it aside. In fact, you may want to tape the shield down, if it gets in your way.

Step 3: Diagnose Any Problems

Your RAM modules (see Figure 22-2) should have white ID stickers identifying their maker and model. Take a minute to write down this information; you're going to need it later.

Figure 22-2

The white ID sticker contains critical info.

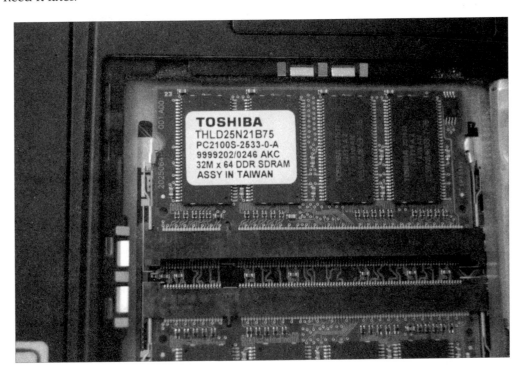

TOSHIBA
THLD25N21B75
PC2100S-2533-0-A
9999202/0246 AKC
32M x 64 DDR SDRAM
ASSY IN TAIWAN

caution *You're going to need to do some research online in the next step. If the laptop you're currently doing surgery on is your one and only computer, put the RAM back in and close up the hatch. You'll have to repeat Step 2 after you're done going online. If you have access to another PC, then proceed.*

Find the Right RAM

Most laptops use a standard type of RAM, making it fairly easy to find compatible modules. The major memory manufacturers, such as Kingston Technology (www.kingston.com) and Crucial Technology (www.crucial.com), offer handy tools on their respective web sites to help you find the right replacement RAM for your laptop. And, of course, they'd be more than happy to *sell* the RAM to you, too. We'll plug our laptop's make and model into Crucial's configurator (see Figure 22-3).

Figure 22-3

Get the scoop on
your RAM.

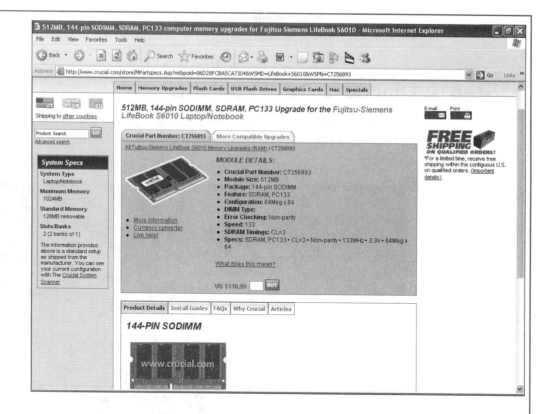

Laptop RAM generally falls into two major types: *Synchronous Dynamic Random Access Memory* (SDRAM) and *Double Data Rate* (DDR). Chances are your machine uses one or the other. Without getting into too many details, you need to make sure that your replacement RAM is of the same type (for example, DDR) and has the same number of pins (for example, 144-pin) as your original RAM.

Most modern laptops have one or two RAM slots, each of which is able to accommodate, at most, a 1 GB RAM chip; although there are exceptions, most laptops can hold a maximum of 2 GB of RAM, which is plenty for all but the most demanding hardcore gamers, video editors, and evil geniuses.

In upgrading our laptop to 1 GB of RAM, we can either add two 512 MB modules or a single 1 GB strip. The former is slightly less expensive; the latter provides slightly better performance (and leaves a slot open for additional, future upgrades). Another option is to leave in one of the original 128 MB modules, and replace the other with a 512 MB module, for a total of 640 MB.

Step 4: Out with the Old...

OK, back to the action. You're about to remove the RAM, but before you do, make double-sure that you're free of static electricity.

Now, using the eraser end of a pencil, gently press the spring-loaded tabs at the tops and bottoms of the memory modules (see Figure 22-4).

Figure 22-4

Press the tabs to release the RAM.

The RAM modules should pop up (see Figure 22-5). If the modules offer any resistance on the way out, snap them back into place and try again. Do not force them or treat them roughly. Once you've got the RAM out, put it in the other plastic baggie.

Figure 22-5

Pop the old chips out.

You probably won't want that old RAM again, but you never know—someone else might need a 128 MB module or two. (You can put it up for sale on eBay, but don't expect to get much for it.) Burned or scorched RAM may indicate that your laptop has a ventilation problem; refer to Project 19 for tips on cleaning your laptop.

Step 5: … In with the New

Time to snap the new RAM modules into place. Match up the short and long rows of connection pins and gently slide the module in, making sure it sits squarely. It's almost impossible to put RAM in backwards, so if you feel resistance, take the module out, and try again. When it's in place, push down gently and the tabs will snap shut, locking it in place.

Step 6: Close Up Shop

OK, it's time to put your laptop back together again. Put the hatch back in place, and screw it shut (see Figure 22-6).

Figure 22-6

Close up the hatch.

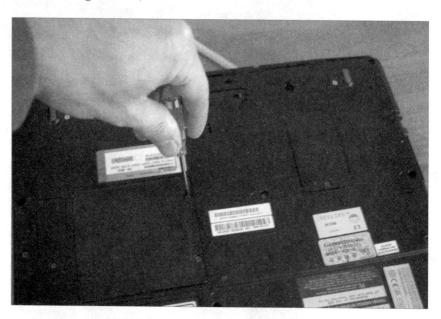

Step 7: Fire it Up

Turn the laptop on. After Windows has loaded, run the CPU-Z utility again. Your new RAM should show up in the Size box on the Memory tab. Make sure that all of the specs listed in the Timings section of the Memory tab (FSB:DRAM ratio, clock cycles) are the same as they were before the upgrade (see Figure 22-7). If they're not—that's not good. You may have gotten a mislabeled module; get in touch with the RAM manufacturer for a replacement.

Step 8: Tune Up the Memory

Running a memory tune-up every month or so will ensure that your new RAM is living up to its potential. The RAM Optimizer from AceLogiX, available for free at www .download.com, is a great utility. Download it, unzip the program, and install the file.

Figure 22-7

Make sure your Timings are the same as before.

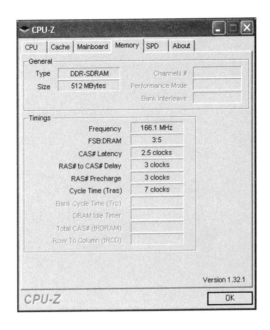

The utility appears as a small, green taskbar icon (see Figure 22-8). Right-click on the icon, select the *Automatic* option from the context menu, sit back, and watch it free up your memory.

Figure 22-8

The RAM Optimizer will free up gobs of memory.

Project 23

Upgrade Your Hard Drive

What You'll Need

- Hardware: Replacement hard drive, USB hard drive enclosure and cable, plastic baggies, Phillips screwdriver or torque wrench
- Software: Windows operating system reinstallation disks
- Cost: $50 to $125 U.S.

If your basement is full of junk and your garage is packed with stuff, you know how frustrating it can be to run out of storage space. Even if you're an uptight neat freak, eventually your laptop will run out of storage space. This is especially true when more and more of people's music, pictures, and movies are stored on their hard drives.

Fortunately, it's a lot easier to replace your laptop's hard drive than it is to add a new basement or expand the garage. Even better, most laptops use a standard 2.5-inch hard drive (see Figure 23-1), making it fairly easy to find compatible replacements.

Some older models use clunky 3.5-inch desktop drives, some tiny models use 1.8-inch drives, and some newer models use a new type of hard drive that has a tiny circuit board in place of the standard 21-pin connector (see Figure 23-2). Whatever type of hard drive your laptop uses, you'll need to find a replacement drive of the same type.

caution *Replacing your hard drive is a fairly simple procedure. Because all of your precious data lives on the hard disk, however, you mess around with it at your own peril. Before you begin this project, we recommend that you back up all of your data (for guidance on how to do this, refer to Project 14).*

Once you've installed the new hard drive, you'll still be able to access your old drive using an external USB enclosure.

So, if your hard drive has grown unreliable, makes odd noises, or is just too small to hold your ever-growing collection of music, photos, or movies, you've come to the right place.

Figure 23-1

The 2.5-inch hard drive is the standard among notebooks.

Figure 23-2

Make sure your replacement matches the original. Here, you can see an older ATA (AT attachment) drive on the right, and a newer Serial ATA drive on the left.

Step 1: Identify Your Drive

If you don't already know what type of hard drive your laptop's got, the first step is to find out. The easiest way to do that is to look at it. That's right; it's time for surgery.

Shut your laptop down. Unplug it. Take the battery out. Give it a minute or two. Before you open it up, your laptop needs to be fully off; listen to make sure the fans have stopped spinning.

Turn your laptop over, so you're facing the underside. The hard drive is located behind a small panel that's often marked by an icon—usually a cylinder or a few overlapping circles. Unscrew the panel (see Figure 23-3), put the screws into a plastic baggie so you don't lose them, and pop the cover off.

Figure 23-3

Open the hatch to get to the hard drive.

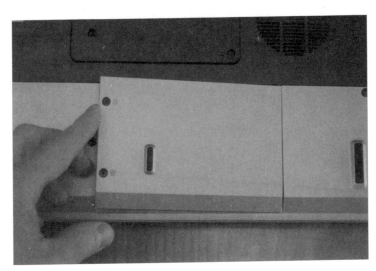

Step 2: Remove the Drive from the Cage

Some hard drives are screwed into a cage that holds them in place (see Figure 23-4).

Figure 23-4

The cage keeps the drive in place.

Others are held in a small, metal envelope (see Figure 23-5).

Figure 23-5

Some drives are held inside a metal sleeve.

Either way, gently remove the hard drive and put it aside.

Step 3: Find the Right Hard Drive

Laptop hard drives come in a variety of sizes and speeds; generally, from 30 to 120 GB of capacity and spinning at one of three speeds—4,200, 5,400, or 7,200 rotations per minute. You're going through the trouble of upgrading, so we recommend that you go big—and the bigger the better; a 120 GB drive doesn't weigh much more than a 30 GB one. Though a faster hard drive will let your laptop retrieve data more quickly, it will also drain your battery much faster than a slower one—and cost a lot more, too. Of course, it's up to you, but we prefer power-efficient 4,200 rpm or 5,400 rpm drives.

There are many places to buy replacement hard drives including online retailers, electronics superstores, and computer specialty stores. And although we're big fans of saving money, we recommend that you don't buy a used drive—it's just not worth the risk.

caution *You may need to use your laptop to format your new hard drive in the next step. If the laptop you're currently doing surgery on is your one and only computer, put the hard drive back in and close up the hatch. You'll have to repeat the first two steps after you're done going online. If you have access to another PC, then proceed.*

Formatting a Hard Drive

If your replacement hard drive comes unformatted, you'll need to format it yourself before you can install it. To do this, you'll need an external hard drive enclosure, which will let you connect the new hard drive to your laptop—or any other PC—for formatting.

Connect the hard drive to the enclosure, and then connect the enclosure to a PC with a USB cable. Open Windows Explorer, right-click on the new hard drive, and select *Format* (see Figure 23-6) to open the *Format* dialog box. Assign the drive a name and pick the formatting scheme; we suggest NTFS, which is faster and more efficient than FAT 32 or FAT 16. Ignore the warning—that everything on the drive will be destroyed—because it's already blank. It'll take somewhere between a half an hour to an hour to format.

Figure 23-6

Your replacement drive must be formatted before you can use it.

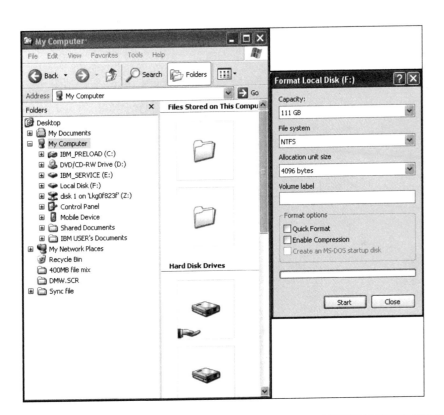

Step 4: Install the New Drive

To install the new hard drive in your laptop, you'll need to reverse the first two steps in this chapter—either reconnect the drive to the cage or put it back into its metal envelope. Whatever you do, be careful not to bend the drive's connection pins (see Figure 23-7).

Figure 23-7

Gently insert the drive
pins into the connector.

Now screw the access panel back on to the underside of the laptop.

Step 5: Get Your Windows Back

Your new hard drive is in, but this project isn't quite done, because your operating
system was on that old hard drive you just took out. Before you turn your laptop back
on, insert the Windows operating system reinstallation CD or DVD that came with
your laptop (see Figure 23-8).

Figure 23-8

Load up your OS
restore media.

Turn your laptop on. The installation process should start automatically. If you have an older laptop, you may need to tweak the BIOS settings to have it boot from the optical drive (see the note below).

note *To change your BIOS settings, start your computer and keep your eyes peeled; before Windows starts, your laptop will display some startup information and offer you a chance to change the BIOS settings. You'll have to press a key—usually F2 or F4, quickly, now—before Windows starts. Once inside the inner sanctum of your computer, you'll see something like Boot Order or Drives. You'll need to configure it so that the optical drive is at the top of the list.*

It'll take an hour or so to reinstall Windows onto the drive.

tip *Once your laptop is back online, check the manufacturers' web site for firmware updates and the Microsoft web site for software, patches, and driver updates.*

Step 6: Check Your Space

You're almost finished. Open Windows Explorer, and right-click on the new hard drive; select *Properties.* You'll see how much free space you've got (see Figure 23-9).

Figure 23-9

See all of your new storage space.

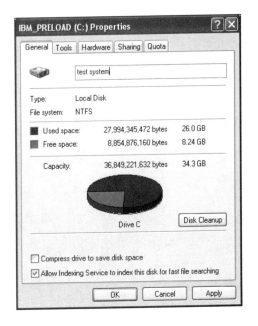

Don't worry if it's a few gigabytes less than you thought; hard drive makers describe their devices' capacity optimistically, while Windows calculates it more pessimistically. And, of course, Windows itself eats up some hard drive space.

Step 7: In with the Old

It's time to move your old data to your new drive. If you saved your data to a CD or DVD or used an external hard drive, it's easy. If not, put your old hard drive into the external enclosure and connect it to your laptop via USB. Drag whichever files you want to keep onto your new drive.

Step 8: Bring Back Those Apps

Now, grab all those old installation CDs and reinstall all of your applications. Once you've installed whatever software you had on your old drive, your laptop should look much as it did before—only with way more free hard drive space.

> **tip** *This is an excellent time to take stock and reinstall only those programs that you actually use. Go through the discs and ask yourself a simple question: "Do I need these?"*

Step 9: Check for Errors

Finally, we recommend that you run Windows' error-checking utility to make sure all of the new drive's sectors are ready to write on; right-click on the hard drive in Explorer, and choose Properties | Tools | Check Now. Go ahead and set the software to automatically repair any bad sectors it encounters.

Upgrade Your Processor

What You'll Need

- Hardware: Replacement CPU, Phillips screwdriver, compressed air, silver thermal paste
- Software: CPU-Z (optional)
- Cost: $100 U.S. or more

Your brain is in your head. Your laptop's brain, also known as its central processing unit, or CPU, lies somewhere underneath its keyboard. While fiddling with your own brain can be a perilous undertaking, replacing your laptop's CPU is eminently doable. That said, it's a delicate business that requires a combination of guts and patience—you'll be messing around with your laptop's most delicate electronics.

caution *Not all laptops are cut out for brain surgery: Many have CPUs that are soldered to other components and can be changed only by tech professionals. If you're unsure whether your laptop's CPU is fixed or not, contact the manufacturer and ask.*

At the point of sale, many laptop makers will try to sell you on the fact that processor speed is the final word in performance. And while it's true that the processor is often the single most expensive component in your laptop, the size and speed of your RAM and hard drive are equally important; for more information about upgrading those components, see Projects 22 and 23.

caution *Full disclosure: A faster processor will cut down on your laptop's battery life.*

Step 1: Find Your CPU

Every laptop's processor is hidden in a different place, though they're all *somewhere* under that keyboard. The manual that came with your laptop may include a schematic drawing with the locations of the major components marked.

Find the Right CPU

You can't just put any old processor into your laptop—though it can be faster, it needs to be electrically identical to the old one. Forget about exchanging that beat-up Pentium III for a Core 2 Duo CPU; it won't work.

To find a replacement CPU, figure out what type you have now (Athlon 64 or Pentium III, for example) and then find out what other speeds it comes in—usually measured in megahertz (MHz) or gigahertz (GHz). Do this sitting down: New CPUs can be very, very expensive.

Find out what other speeds are available for your processor type. Take note that a *much* faster processor may need an additional or higher power fan to keep it from melting down. Do not replace your processor with one designed for a desktop PC; the voltages are probably different, it will produce much more heat, and if it even works, it'll drain your battery in mere moments.

Here are a few good online resources for finding a replacement CPU:

- **InfoHQ.com:** Page 4 of InfoHQ's laptop buying guide includes a comprehensive list of processor types and speeds.

- **You laptop manufacturer's web site.**

- **Sparepartswarehouse.com:** Offering a good selection of CPUs, often for less than the manufacturer's charge; the company requires you to turn in your old CPU.

If your manual doesn't help, after your laptop is warmed up, feel around for a hot spot; the processor probably lies somewhere beneath. If you can't find a hot spot, just open up the access panel on the underside of your laptop that's closest to the fans (see Figure 24-1).

Figure 24-1

The processor is hiding behind one of those panels.

If you don't see any fans, forget it—we'll go in blind. Pick a panel and open it up.

 Some manufacturers don't bother to include access panels. That means you're going to need to take out the keyboard to get at the CPU. Good luck.

Step 2: Seek the Sink

You're looking for the shiny, copper-colored heat sink (see Figure 24-2), which absorbs and dissipates heat from the processor. Once you've found it, congratulations! You're in the right place.

Figure 24-2

Found the copper-colored heat sink? You're getting warm!

Step 3: Extract the Sink

The heat sink is generally connected to the processor with special, spring-loaded screws. Use a Phillips head screwdriver to loosen and remove them. Be careful; the springs may fly off, and you're going to need them to connect your new processor to the heat sink.

Step 4: Separate the CPU and Heat Sink

Gently separate the heat sink from the CPU (see Figure 24-3). The thermal paste used to attach them may have become hard and rigid, so you'll have to apply some pressure to pry them apart. Be careful: the CPU is extremely delicate.

Figure 24-3

The heat sink (left) and
processor stand (right).

Figure 24-3

The heat sink (left) and
processor stand (right).

Step 5: Out with the Old Brain...

With the heat sink removed, use your finger to unlock the handle on the side of the
CPU socket (see Figure 24-4).

Figure 24-4

Pull the handle to
loosen the CPU.

This will release the processor's connection pins. You should now be able to lift it
out vertically (see Figure 24-5). If it doesn't budge or gets stuck, wiggle it a little bit.
Put the old CPU aside: one way or another, you're likely to need it.

Figure 24-5

Remove the CPU and
put it in a safe place.

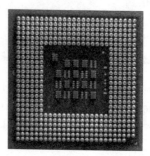

Step 6: Cleanup Time

Time to return our attention to the heat sink. Spray it clean with a can of compressed air; if you don't have compressed air, use a synthetic cloth to give it a good cleaning, removing any accumulated dust and lint.

Now, put some acetone or fingernail polish remover on the end of a cotton swab and rub off the dried, silver thermal paste from the surface of the heat sink. Make sure that there's no debris on the side of the heat sink that will come into contact with the CPU (see Figure 24-6).

Figure 24-6

Make your heat sink sparkle!

Step 7: ...In with The New Brain

Take the new CPU and put it side by side with the old one. The pins should match up exactly. If not, you'll need a different replacement CPU; refer back to *Find the Right CPU* at the beginning of this chapter.

Step 8: Spread It on Thick

Spread a generous gob of silver thermal paste on both the CPU and the heat sink (see Figure 24-7).

Figure 24-7

A little dab will do ya'.

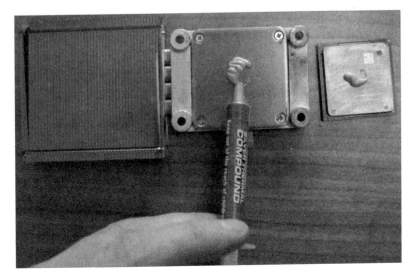

Using the spreader that came with the paste (or, alternatively, the corner of a business card), smooth the paste out on the CPU and heat sink (see Figure 24-8).

Figure 24-8

Now spread it out.

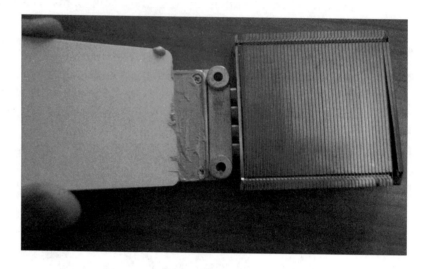

You want a nice, even coat on each surface.

> **tip** *A few words about working with thermal paste. Look for a paste that's at least 50 percent silver content (by weight), and when you apply it, wear gloves or, in a pinch, a plastic bag on your hands; while it isn't dangerous to work with, it is quite gooey and messy. For any thermal paste-related accidents, acetone cleans it up rather well.*

Step 9: Socket to Me

Now it's time to put the replacement CPU back into its socket. Both the CPU and the socket each have a corner without pins; start by lining up those corners. Now, with the thermal paste side facing up, gently push the CPU straight down (see Figure 24-9). It should slide in smoothly. Lock the handle in place.

> **tip** *If the processor puts up a fight going into the socket, take it back out and examine it for dirt or debris. Inspect the pins to see if any have been bent; if so, you have two options. You can use a small pair of pliers to very carefully straighten them out. Or you can put the CPU halfway into the socket, just enough for all the pins to seat, and then slowly close and open the locking handle. This can sometimes straighten out bent pins.*

Step 10: Attach the Heat Sink

Next, attach the heat sink. Squish the two together, so the thermal paste blends, and then screw it down using the spring-loaded bolts (see Figure 24-10).

Wipe up any excess paste with a cloth.

Figure 24-9

Put the new CPU
in place.

Figure 24-10

Screw it all back
together.

Step 11: Put It All Back Together

Reattach the access panel.

Step 12: Turn It On!

Turn on your laptop. If it works, that's good. Congratulations!

If the laptop won't start, go back to Step 9 and make sure the CPU is secured snugly into the socket.

tip *Assess your new CPU speed with CPU-Z, a free utility available at www.cpuid.com. Download the software, unzip it, and double-click the icon to run the program. CPU-Z will cough up a lot of information about your laptop's components and performance parameters, including your CPU speed.*

OK, the transplant is complete. Go wipe that silver thermal paste off your hands and enjoy your laptop's new brain.

Index